Edible and Medicinal Plants of the West

Edible and Medicinal Plants of the West

Gregory L. Tilford

With a Foreword by Michael Moore

Mountain Press Publishing Company
Missoula, Montana
1997

Printed in Hong Kong by Mantec Production Company

Library of Congress Cataloging-in-Publication Data

Tilford, Gregory L.
  Edible and medicinal plants of the West / Gregory L. Tilford; with
a foreword by Michael Moore.
     p.   cm.
  Includes bibliographical references and index.
  ISBN 0-87842-359-1.   (alk. paper)
  1. Wild plants, Edible—West (U.S.) 2. Wild plants, Edible—Canada,
Western. 3. Medicinal plants—West (U.S.) 4. Medicinal plants—Canada,
Western. 5. Wild plants, Edible—West (U.S.)—Pictorial works. 6. Wild
plants, Edible—Canada, Western—Pictorial works. 7. Medicinal plants—
West (U.S.)—Pictorial works. 8. Medicinal plants—Canada, Western—
Pictorial works.   I. Title.
QK98.5.U6T54   1997
581.6'3'0978—dc21   97-842
                                                    CIP

Mountain Press Publishing Company
P.O. Box 2399 • Missoula, MT 59806
406-728-1900

Disclaimer

My intent in this book is to provide plant profiles that inform the reader through recorded scientific and empirical data. It reflects the theories, histories, and, to no small degree, the author's personal opinions and speculations surrounding the usefulness of wild plants. Although many of the plants described are in clinical, therapeutic use around the world, this book represents only a cursory introduction to plant medicines and edible wild plants in western North America. It is not intended as a substitute for the skills of a qualified health care practitioner or nutritional consultant. I strongly urge readers to seek professional advice before using any plant medicines or wild foods.

The use of wild plants as food or medicine demands a strong measure of common sense. Many of the plants described in this book are strong medicines and some are poisonous. They deserve a high degree of respect. One book or even a dozen books are insufficient to convey the knowledge a person needs to safely and responsibly use wild plants. Looking at pictures in a book is only the beginning and is no substitute for examining plants in the wild. With this and the subject of common sense in mind, I recommend hands-on field training with a qualified professional in the proper identification and use of wild plants before engaging in harvest for any level of ingestion or therapeutic use. Consult a qualified health care practitioner before using plants as foods or medicines.

The author, publisher, bookseller, and anyone else associated with the distribution of this book assume no liability for the actions of the reader.

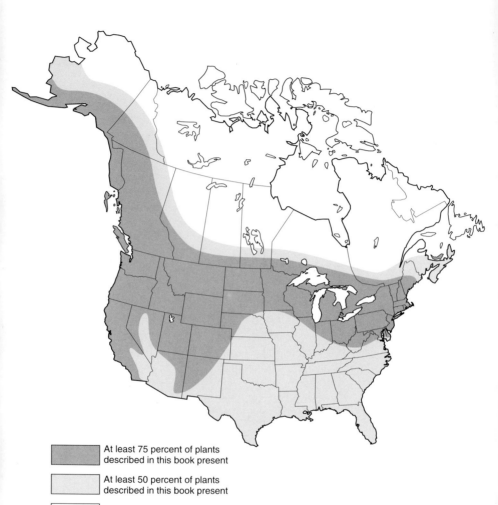

At least 75 percent of plants
described in this book present

At least 50 percent of plants
described in this book present

Less than 50 percent of plants
described in this book present

The Area Covered in This Book

Although a few of the plants in this book grow exclusively in the deserts and coastal canyons of the United States Southwest, the book's central focus extends from the northern Rocky Mountains bioregion to the coastal ranges of the Pacific Northwest, including northern California, Oregon, Washington, Idaho, Montana, Alaska, British Columbia, and southern Alberta.

At least 75 percent of the plants described here can be found in appropriate habitats and ecological niches throughout the Rocky Mountains south to the inland and coastal mountains of California, Arizona, Nevada, and New Mexico, and throughout the temperate coniferous forests of the northern third of North America to the eastern shores of the Great Lakes.

More than half of the plants presented in this book grow wild or in cultivation throughout the remaining parts of the United States.

Contents

Foreword *xi*

Acknowledgments *xiii*

Introduction *1*
Humble Beginnings and Ancient Allies *1*
The Green Revolution *3*
Scope and Purpose of This Book *4*
How to Use This Book *6*
Toxicity *8*
Commonsense Guidelines *9*

Part I: Edible and Medicinal Plants *11*

Alder *12*
Alumroot *12*
Amaranth *14*
American Speedwell *14*
Arrowleaf Balsamroot *16*
Beargrass *16*
Bee Balm *18*
Bistort *18*
Blue Camas *20*
Buffalo Berry *20*
Bugleweed *22*
Bunchberry *22*
Burdock *24*
California Poppy *26*
Cascara Sagrada *26*
Catnip *28*
Cattail *28*
Chickweed *30*
Chicory *32*
Chiming Bells *32*
Chokecherry *34*
Cleavers *36*
Coltsfoot *38*
Coptis *40*
Cow Parsnip *42*
Cranesbill Geranium *42*
Creosote Bush or Chaparral *44*
Currant *46*

Dandelion *48*
Devil's Club *50*
Echinacea *52*
Elderberry *54*
Evening Primrose *56*
False Solomon's Seal *58*
Field Mint *60*
Filaree *60*
Fireweed *62*
Glacier Lily *64*
Goldenrod *66*
Ground Ivy *68*
Harebell *68*
Hawthorn *70*
Heal-All *70*
Hedge Nettle *72*
Henbit *72*
Horehound *74*
Horsetail *76*
Hound's Tongue *78*
Huckleberry *80*
Indian Paintbrush *82*
Juniper *84*
Kinnikinnick *86*
Knapweed *88*
Lamb's Quarter *88*
Licorice *90*
Lousewort *92*

Maidenhair Fern *94*
Mallow *94*
Meadowsweet *96*
Milkweed *96*
Monkeyflower *98*
Miner's Lettuce *98*
Motherwort *100*
Mullein *102*
Nettle-Leafed Horsemint *102*
Oregon Grape *104*
Oxeye Daisy *106*
Pearly Everlasting *108*
Periwinkle *108*
Pineapple Weed *110*
Pipsissewa *110*
Plantain *112*
Poplar *114*
Prickly Lettuce *116*
Prickly-Pear Cactus *118*
Pyrola *120*
Raspberry *122*
Red Clover *124*
Red Osier Dogwood *124*
Red Root *126*
Sage *128*
Saint John's Wort *130*
Salal *132*

Salsify *132*
Serviceberry *134*
Sheep Sorrel *134*
Skullcap *136*
Shootingstar *136*
Spring Beauty *138*
Stonecrop *140*
Sweetroot *142*
Thistle *144*
Twisted-Stalk *146*
Usnea Lichen *148*
Valerian *150*
Violet *152*
Watercress *154*
Waterleaf *154*
Wild Ginger *156*
Wild Mustards *158*
Wild Onion *160*
Wild Rose *162*
Wild Strawberry *162*
Willow *164*
Yampa *166*
Yarrow *166*
Yellow Bells *168*
Yellow Dock *168*
Yerba Santa *170*
Yucca *172*

Part II: Toxic Plants and Advanced Medicines *175*

Angelica *178*
Arnica *180*
Baneberry *182*
Biscuitroot *184*
Bittersweet *186*
Black Henbane *186*
Castor Bean *188*
Clematis *190*
Columbine *192*
Death Camas *194*
Dogbane *196*

False Hellebore *198*
Gromwell *198*
Hemlock Parsley *200*
Jimsonweed *202*
Osha *204*
Pasqueflower *206*
Sagebrush *208*
Stinging Nettle *210*
Tansy *212*
Water Hemlock *214*

Glossary *217*

Bibliography and Recommended Reading *225*

Index *227*

Foreword

There's a sentiment shared by old geezer sci-fi fans: Back when they were kids, they read a short story by Campbell or a novel by Heinlein that gave them a "sense of wonder"—a feeling of inexplicable, creepy joy that, over the years, kept them reading science fiction. They judged what they read by the author's ability to rekindle the ancient and often fading sense of awe.

I have been a professional herbalist for nearly thirty years now, and I still remember my first encounter with a plant and that first sense of wonder. The year was probably 1967. I had a field guide and a couple of herb books with me when I came across a field of yarrow in bloom, somewhere below the top of Mt. Piños in Ventura County, California. I gathered the flowering heads (marveling at their smell), took them back to my home in North Hollywood, and dried them in a big wicker basket. I did what the books recommended: I made tea and drank it (and sweated); I used it for a hair rinse (and my, even then, receding hair shone); I used it in a bath (and felt relaxed and invigorated).

A small thing, true, but I had been looking for some excuse to get away from Los Angeles, to get into the foothills and mountains, to get away for awhile from my work in the music business and the hordes of fellow humans, all of us chittering about with shallow, rabid intent. I knew I could look for rocks (but why?), look for mammals (they were few and always ran away), or look for birds (more common but even more elusive). The idea of wearing khaki shorts and walking around with a belly pack and a hiking stick, gawking at nature seemed, to my city aesthetics, most absurd. If I wanted to get away from town, I had to be "doing something." Plants at least stood still, came in great variety, and could be used for both food and medicine. Plants did something.

It began with yarrow, followed by manzanita, white sage, California romero, and others. I discovered a world apart from the Local 47 Union Hall on Vine Street, the recording studios on Santa Monica, and the boutiques in Studio City. I found reality in the nonhuman. The foothills no longer were spaces between jobs, but worlds of their own, filled with an increasing number of friends. I had found my own sense of wonder.

Within a year I was packaging and wholesaling herbal products; within two years I had opened an herb store. I retailed and wholesaled herbs for the next twenty years. For the past twenty years, I have taught regularly on the use and identification of plants. Every class allows me to share the wonder and rekindle it within myself.

There is something innately empowering and subversive about the ability to find your own food and medicine. It goes against the nature of current American culture. In a world of increased complexity, it is simple. Amid sophisticated and often arcane marketing, it is completely generic. While the manufacturing and distribution of food has been removed from sight, the gathering of at least some of your food is homely and pure. While standard-practice medicine is dissolving into a morass of steely and sometimes inhuman complexity, plant remedies can allow a person to treat lesser health complaints and begin to relearn the simple flesh-wisdom of "little sick" (take some teas, sweat it out, moan and groan, and get better quicker) and "big sick" (get your ass to a doctor already!).

Greg Tilford wrote *Edible and Medicinal Plants of the West* with all this in mind. He explains with care and intelligence the value of gathering some of your food, the benefits of moderate and careful use of self-gathered remedies, and then takes you carefully through the steps of differential identification and sensible and ethical gathering and preparation. He invites us to view ourselves as part of the biosphere from which we harvest, and encourages us to take this sense of wonder back to town with us.

I have often stopped to wonder why the growing hordes of urban and rural "survivalists" spend so much time buying really cool knives, oiling their marginally illegal armaments, and passing antiauthoritarian gossip around like a bunch of tongue-clucking fishwives. True survival rests not in the big macho stances, but in the gentler arts of knowing one's natural world and knowing how to use it in a moral and renewable fashion.

Greg Tilford offers us usable information in this manual, good descriptions and photographs. He presumes we have brains, sensibilities, and intelligence. He leaves us with the beginnings of a true craft—and a sense of wonder.

Michael Moore
November 1996
Bisbee, Arizona

Acknowledgments

Many people have had a positive influence on this book, and acknowledging all of them is difficult. A few names, however, stand out.

First, I once again thank Mary Wulff-Tilford, my wife, teacher, and primary herbalist mentor, for her patience and insight throughout this project. She is the one who lit the herbal fire in me years ago. Without her, this book would not exist.

I thank Kathy Lloyd, Drake Barton, and all my herbalist students for the energy and motivation that have inspired me as a teacher and a writer through the years.

Thanks to all of my herbalist teachers and colleagues: Michael Moore, David Hoffmann, James Green, Rosemary Gladstar, Ed Smith, Richo Cech, Robyn Klein, and everyone else who has prompted me to keep looking deeper into the world of plants.

To my brothers of heart and spirit, Terry Aleck (Coyote 7) of the Nlha7kapmx Nation and Davi´d, the two great medicine men who helped illuminate my path in life by treating me to the sight of an eagle.

My special thanks to Ken Allaman, whose friendship and photographic expertise helped me with many of the key photographic techniques I used for this book.

And especially, a reverent thank-you to the plants, animals, and wonders of nature that fill my heart with the warm glow of a curious child.

Introduction

Humble Beginnings and Ancient Allies

When we view our universe at the most rudimentary level, we see that all things are composed of energy, and for something to be alive, its collective energy must be continually fed and replenished. Plants provide a critical, life-giving link between what is alive and what is not. Without plants, sunlight could not be transformed into usable energy, and life as we know it could not exist. Through the process of photosynthesis, plants take energy from the sun and convert it into chlorophyll, the basis of assimilable energy that allows the perpetuation and continuance of the food chain. Plants also supply our planet with oxygen, and according to their specific molecular structures, they provide all life with the specialized energetic actions we refer to as medicines.

Animals are the oldest herbalists on earth, and most of what we know about medicine began during prehistoric times, with observations of them and their intuitive uses of plants. It probably all started when humans, too, were intuitive creatures, with the first person who instinctively ingested a plant and discovered that it made him or her feel better. Historic sites in Iraq suggest that Neanderthals used healing herbs such as yarrow and marshmallow 60,000 years ago (Castleman, 1991). From that point on, each success encouraged further experimentation, and the sciences of medicine were born through the dangerous hardships of trial and error.

With each new generation, the collective body of human intellect grew through experience, and eventually, instinct began yielding to a reasoning human mind. We learned to observe how animals maintain well-being from the plants they eat, and from this (and more trial and error) we began to adapt their inherent abilities to our benefit.

As the eons passed, people developed a deep respect for plants and animals, regarding many of them as sacred couriers of well-being. They took on new meaning and were no longer viewed solely as objective food sources but as divine offerings yielding health and wisdom. Tribal healers earned powerful status as spiritual leaders and liaisons between plants, animals, and the spirit world. Through the insights of the "wise woman" or "medicine man," people around the world recognized that the healing and nutritive powers of plants were deeply connected to the welfare of the land that yielded them. The earth was revered as a sacred body of life. Many early cultures, including those of Native Americans, believed that the human species was not a separate entity that walked upon the earth but rather an integral part of a huge, living organism. Some cultures call

1

this organism "Gaia," meaning "the living earth." This philosophy views food and healing in a broad perspective far beyond the needs of the human self. It sees the entire human condition as a humble segment of the universal scheme, where everything is related. To live by this philosophy means to realize and accept that the maintenance of a healthy human mind, body, and spirit is critically dependent on the maintenance of good health in our planet. In this context, the herbalists and food-gatherers of prehistoric times not only were physicians but also caretakers of the earth.

Eventually, humanity lost its patience in nature's classroom. Things in nature do not happen fast enough for us. As our brains developed so did the complexity of our questions and our appetite for immediate answers. By 3400 B.C., Chinese explorer Shen Nung had compiled the first herbal reference, which cataloged over 234 medicinal herbs (Castleman, 1991). Humans began to rationalize the universe; science and technology were born, and with each scientific success we became increasingly confident that we could take more control of the natural universe to exploit its powers. Hunting and gathering gave way to farming and ranching as we developed new breeds of livestock and food crops that grew bigger, faster, and more abundantly than those provided in nature. Around A.D. 1300, various religious and government influences began grappling for a disproportionate share of power. Governing clergies perceived earth- or nature-oriented philosophies as pagan and regarded such beliefs as threatening to their standards of control and order. With no small measure of violence, people eventually were compelled to forget many of the old ways and were forced to adopt lifestyles chosen by their hierarchies. This is particularly true in Western cultures, where spiritualism is largely separated from medicine. Perhaps this is unfortunate, for as we consider the environmental damage and social chaos we have caused we must wonder what insightful gifts may have been surrendered at the expense of our burgeoning sciences.

The link between herbalism and the environment has been lost in most cultures, but herbal medicine has survived. Most Eastern cultures (the bulk of the world population) still use botanicals in their mainstream practices of medicine. In China, where organized herbal medicine dates back at least 5,000 years, herbs are still used according to ancient methods, and they have been integrated with modern Western technologies. To the Chinese, Western medicine is the alternative choice of healing, as it is throughout India and most of Asia.

So what happened in the West?

Herbalism is nothing new to North America. Botanical medicines comprised two-thirds of the United States pharmacopoeia until 1820 and continued as the primary means of healing until the turn of the century. Roughly 40 percent of all drugs in modern use are derived from plants, and many drugs that are synthetically produced today were born from botanical sources. In Latin America, modern-day folkloric healers continue to earn the respect of the general populous, and herbs predominate in mainstream practices and drugstores (botanicas).

More than 70 percent of botanically derived drugs in North America were discovered from folkloric accounts, and the major pharmaceutical companies spend millions of dollars each year in worldwide research of the "old ways." A study by the Drug Research and Development Branch of the National Cancer Institute

2

examined 70,000 extracts from 7,500 plant species and concluded that 750 of them possessed antitumor properties. Of thousands of North American plant species that have been randomly studied by medical researchers, 40 percent have been found to have immune-stimulating properties. Several wild plants have recently shown great promise in treating HIV, hepatitis, herpes, various forms of virus, bacterial infections, tuberculosis, chronic depression, diabetes, and hundreds of other diseases.

Despite it all, Western science largely shuns herbal medicine. Why? The reasons stem from politics, economics, and good ol' greed.

It all began about seventy-five years ago with the discovery of antibiotics, vaccines, and other heroic forms of medicine. The nearly immediate, seemingly miraculous results of these medicines quickly captured everyone's interest, and Western medicine took on a distinctly symptomatic approach to healing. Unlike herbal therapies, which focus on *supporting* the natural disease-fighting functions of the body, Western science takes an allopathic and symptomatic approach to medicine, where drugs are designed to *interfere* with body functions to effect more immediate results. With the advent of antibiotics, vaccines, and advanced surgical intervention, therapies that once took months to reach symptomatic results now took only days, sometimes only hours. Everybody wanted to reap the convenient rewards of the new "miracle drugs." Western medicine abandoned prevention in favor of the quick fix, and a huge and politically powerful pharmaceutical industry erupted almost overnight. Botanical medicines soon were no longer in the medical research limelight.

Today, modern medicine represents a multibillion-dollar industry in America, and given the nature of today's political and economic structure, it would be unrealistic to assume that the dandelions in your backyard will ever receive anything but a cold shoulder from the pharmaceutical industry. Though tremendous amounts of time and money have gone into botanical research (particularly in Europe and Asia) to validate the efficacy of herbal medicines, it is unlikely that economic powers in America will quietly relinquish control of their monopolies to favor weeds, which many people could freely access. Also, the cost of researching a new drug for Food and Drug Administration (FDA) approval is in the neighborhood of $200 million.

Many people are tiring of this costly, greedy way of life. As a result, many of the old ways are being renewed.

The Green Revolution

As we enter a new millennium, many aspects of our technological age are backfiring. We are beginning to see a collapse of the human immune system as our modern "miracle drugs" are failing to combat some of the diseases they were originally designed to fight. Many strains of bacteria have become resistant to antibiotics, and the allopathic options are dwindling. Viruses both new and old are popping up everywhere on earth. The use of vaccines and preventative antibiotic therapies is raising heated controversies among physicians and medical researchers, who now argue the long-term effects these drugs may have on our bodies. Food crops, all originally wild plants, are becoming more and more depleted of nutrients as we continue to alter them genetically to meet the supply and demand of our exploding population. Spinach, for instance, has only 5 to 15 percent the nutritional value it had in 1950, even when grown organically.

Maybe the Gaia perspective holds true. Perhaps hundreds of years of environmental abuse and human consumption have thrown our planet so far out of balance that nature has begun to slap us across the face. Many of us have felt the sting. Even some of the world's leading scientists, in the absence of scientific solutions, are beginning to theorize that viruses and bacteria may represent the autoimmune soldiers (the white blood cells) of the earth, and humanity represents the infection.

In the midst of these horrors, while the doctors, researchers, and pharmaceutical companies throw up their arms in disbelief or denial, a strong environmental movement is gaining momentum. People are looking into our past for answers, reinvestigating not only the old ways of medicine but the old ways of living and worshiping the earth. A collective scrutiny of the human condition is under way in a race against the consumption of resources, and people in unprecedented numbers are recapturing the holistic perspectives of our ancestors. Medicinal and edible plants are making a comeback in America as millions of people seek healthy, holistic alternatives to mainstream foods and medicines. And as we discover that our ancient allies of well-being are still with us, we see they are more useful than ever—and living as weeds between the rows of their hybrid descendants.

More than 150,000 plant species inhabit the earth. More than 20,000 grow in the western half of North America. But faster than modern herbalists and medical researchers can discover the plant's attributes, many species are vanishing. With each disappearance, we can only speculate about our loss. Only about 15 percent of all known plants have been examined for nutritive and medicinal values, and only a scant number of them have been thoroughly researched.

Many of the plants introduced into North America were brought here by our ancestors as foods or medicines and were forgotten in the wake of science. The healing possibilities they offer are endless. The cure for deadly and debilitating diseases such as cancer and AIDS may be as close as our backyards. Beyond their benefit as food or medicine for our bodies, plants offer us an opportunity to rekindle a connection with earth. Through an appreciation of plants, we can recapture the wisdom of our ancestors and resume a place of harmonious interdependence with our planet.

Scope and Purpose of This Book

This book describes a select few (more than 250 species) of the many edible and medicinal plants of North America. Although a few of the plants in this book grow exclusively in the deserts and coastal canyons of the United States Southwest, the book's central focus extends from the northern Rocky Mountains to the coastal ranges of the Pacific Northwest, including Oregon, Washington, Idaho, Montana, Alaska, and western Canada. Extending from this central focus, at least 75 percent of the plants described here can be found in appropriate habitats throughout the temperate coniferous forests of the northern third of North America to the eastern shores of the Great Lakes and throughout the Rocky Mountains, south into the inland and coastal mountains of California, Arizona, Nevada, and

New Mexico. More than half of the plants presented in this book grow naturally or cultivated throughout the remaining portions of the United States. This is a region of vast and variable geography and rich biodiversity, and deciding which of the thousands of useful plants to focus on was not easy. The history of this region is equally rich, and a comprehensive account of ethnobotanical records would fill several volumes. I have chosen an assortment of species that readers will find useful and important according to their differing needs and interests.

My goals in writing this book are many. First, I was influenced by concerns for our troubled planet and the belief that until we build a deeper awareness of what lies beneath our feet, we can do little to help her. To alter our course from the destructive path we have blazed through the forests of the West, we must first understand how a forest operates—exclusive of our influence. For most people, this seems to be an unreachable goal, for where do we start? After all, as a species we have been concerned only for ourselves for centuries, and aside from our scientific efforts to manage an ecosystem, we have few clues to how an ecosystem naturally operates. It is my heartfelt wish that this book will precipitate a new appreciation of the potential importance each of these plants holds. Whether we use them or not, edible and medicinal plants offer us a wide perspective on the unseen world that lies beneath the trees and above the precious minerals we tend to take for granted. We have the opportunity to learn new levels of respect, and from respect we can learn to love and better protect what has sustained us all along.

My second goal is to fill an educational niche for the wild plant enthusiast. In searching for the ideal field guide to edible and medicinal plants of the West, you quickly realize that a perfect solution cannot exist. Botanical keys present us with the most accurate means of plant identification, but they require a precise familiarity with botanical terminology and taxonomy that discourages the novice and daunts even the most advanced herbologist. Also, most keys require the plants to be in bloom to fulfill their purpose of positive identification; unfortunately, few of us can plan our outings around nature's schedule. At the other end of the spectrum are guidebooks that describe and illustrate edible and medicinal plants using generalities that cannot be relied on for purposes of positive identification (much less for purposes of ingestion). These books have overview photos or artwork that only convey what a plant *might* look like, and their descriptions fall short of conveying anything but the generalities of a species. What they do not address are the specific, often minute nuances that distinguish each plant through sensual mediums beyond appearance. Few guidebooks accurately describe the feel, smell, taste, and behavior of plants.

I am not a formally trained botanist. I am an herbalist and naturalist, and I pursue my knowledge of plants through a legacy of practical, hands-on experience. Being an herbalist, I do not merely appreciate the appearance of plants, *I put them into my body*, a practice that demands an intimate familiarity with them. Any herbalist or wild food forager can tell you that botanical guidelines are not enough to satisfy his or her requirements of positive identification. Like other herbalists, I have learned to recognize my chosen allies by getting my hands dirty and understanding the unique signatures of each plant. Besides following conventional botanical guidelines, I have learned to recognize plants through personalized perceptions and methods of observation that appeal to our individual memories. For example, a plant easily recognized stands out in my memory not by its appearance but by the texture of its leaves. You, however, might find its flowers easier to remember, or its seeds. Perception differs with each individual, and what feels "hairy" to one person may feel "fuzzy" to another. Although scientific, botanical parameters are important in beginning the recognition process, we need not be bound to the perceptions of others when committing a plant to memory.

Much of the intimate knowledge I am referring to relates to hands-on experience and cannot be conveyed in the pages of a book. But a basis for developing your own personalized standards of plant recognition can and will be provided. As in other books about edible and medicinal plants, included here are general descriptions of each plant's appearance and habitat. I have also included the "intimate intricacies" that I find useful as part of each plant's unique signature; for example, the "dirty sock" odor of valerian, the single line of tiny hairs on the stems of chickweed, and the unique leaf veins of fireweed. Think of these references first as tools for stimulating your imagination; then look for plant signatures that appeal to your personal system of memorable familiarity. This exploratory process is fun and is a valuable tool for developing greater perceptive abilities.

For the novice, this book will provide a close-up introduction to hundreds of useful plants of the West, while opening doors to countless possibilities. For the expert, it will provide another, perhaps fresher perspective into the fascinating world of edible and medicinal plants.

How to Use This Book

Headings. This book is designed for easy use by plant enthusiasts at all levels. Each plant description begins with headings giving the plant's most widespread common name (chokecherry), Latin genera and species *(Prunus virginiana)*, common family name (Rose family), and Latin family name (Rosaceae).

Although most plant field guides and botanical keys are compiled in scientific formats that direct the reader to a plant species through step-by-step recognition of botanical order, family, genus, and specific characteristics, I have chosen to list the plants in this book alphabetically by their common names. Though unconventional in scientific books, the simple and recognizable format of this book appeals to varied levels of plant familiarity throughout a broad audience of readers. As you begin to recognize the plants in this book by their common names, I encourage you also to learn their Latin names.

Common names tend to be generic, often referring to several unrelated species. "Indian tobacco," for example, names dozens of unrelated plants throughout the West. "Wintergreen" is not much better. Start learning Latin names—it is not as difficult as you might think. Begin by learning the genus name of each plant. The genus refers to a group of species within a plant family. In many cases, this is all you need to know; learning the exact species (specific member of a genus) can come later.

For purposes of field identification, most people find that remembering plants by family is of little practical use. A family of plants may consist of several thousand genera and species with wide variations. Perhaps the best and biggest example is the Sunflower family (Compositae), which has more than 900 genera and 19,000 species worldwide; many of them look remarkably different from one another. Look at the photos of arrowleaf balsamroot and sagebrush in this book. Both are members of the Sunflower family, and therefore share certain physical characteristics. But for practical purposes of identification, do you see any resemblance?

Plant Descriptions. A general description of each plant includes my personal observations of some of the unique nuances that help define the plant. Wherever possible, close-up photographs further illustrate the identifying characteristics.

I have attempted to describe the physical characteristics of each plant in the simplest terms possible. Some plant characteristics, though, are difficult (if not impossible) to convey with anything but botanical terminology. When you encounter an unfamiliar botanical term, please refer to the glossary. The labeled photo on page 216 illustrates the anatomy of a flower.

Blooms. I have indicated the time period when you will most likely find the plant blooming. Please bear in mind, however, that nature has few absolutes. The flowering cycles of plants are subject to many variables, including microclimates, changes in weather, altitude, latitude (a plant in Canada may bloom later than the same species in Arizona), and other environmental aspects.

Habitat and Range. This section provides broad outlines for each plant's habitat and range in the West. I refer to general ranges because the range of many plants changes constantly with alterations in weather patterns, seed transport by migrating animals, introduction by humans, and countless other influences. Many plants are adaptable to various habitats and constantly mutate or hybridize in their efforts to survive in a changing world.

Edibility. Under this subheading I have listed some of the current and historical food uses of the plant. I have also conveyed some of my personal opinions relative to palatability. Please bear in mind that what may be edible and enjoyable for one person may taste vile or even be poisonous to another. This book is not intended as a definitive guide to what is good food and what is not; it is an introduction to some of the many possibilities.

Toxicity. In Part II, Toxic Plants and Advanced Medicines, I have replaced the Edibility subheading in many of the profiles with "Toxicity." Under this subheading, I provide a general account of the plant's toxicity: why, and to what extent, it is dangerous. Again, what may cause only minor nausea in one person may lead to an ambulance ride for another.

Medicinal Uses. Here I have listed some of the historic and present uses of each plant as a medicine; the accounts may be scientific, empirical, or folkloric. I have also included notes that relate to scientific research, theories, validation, and speculation, with a generous dose of my own thoughts and opinions. This information is not intended to prescribe any specific course of therapy, but is intended to introduce the reader to each plant's potential as a therapeutic device.

Look-Alike Plants. I have included this section (when appropriate and within my knowledge) to inform you of plants that may be confused with the plant being described. Wherever possible, I provide photographic cross-references to assist you in differentiating the look-alike from the subject plant.

Warning! I have described any hazardous aspects (within my knowledge) that you should be aware of relating to the use of each plant. The intent of this book is to educate the reader of the therapeutic and culinary possibilities presented by the plants it describes. This book is not intended to serve as a practical guide to herbal medicines or the use of wild foods. No single book can cover all the issues you need to examine before putting a wild plant to culinary or medicinal use, and no number of books can replace hands-on training with a qualified professional. This book is not a complete source of practical information. This said, if you do employ any of these plants, I strongly recommend that you thoroughly research them through several other mediums, preferably under the personal instruction of an expert. Many excellent resources together can provide a solid foundation of knowledge. To begin your informative quest, I have included a comprehensive bibliography at the back of this book.

Toxicity

Be careful and use common sense. Any plant can be toxic. In fact, life can be toxic. Webster defines a poison as a substance that has a "destructive or harmful influence." Period. Anything we eat, drink, absorb, or do is poisonous if done to excess. Too much running will lead to destruction of connective tissues; too many prunes will disrupt digestive balances in our bodies.

Toxicity, as it relates to our bodies, is directly associated with rate of absorption and our ability to assimilate or eliminate an excess. If the body receives a substance in quantities or concentrations it cannot effectively deal with through its natural functions, the result is a poisoning, which must then be treated by emergency means. Vomiting, diarrhea, and other purgative functions are triggered to eliminate the invasive substance(s). If this fails, systemic shutdown or damage may follow.

I am not bringing this to your attention to discourage you, but to inform you about a few commonsense guidelines before you decide to indulge in the weeds in your backyard. First, be certain of what you are about to ingest. Second, use moderation. Plants, whether the asparagus you buy at the supermarket or chickweed you pull from the flower bed, must be respected by rules of common sense. Too much of *anything* is toxic.

Many critics of wild foods and herbal medicines use the same reductionist methods to discredit herbs from which modern scientists produce lifesaving drugs; in both cases, specific plant chemicals are singled out from the whole plant to achieve a goal. With black henbane (a poisonous plant in any capacity), the alkaloid atropine is singled out from hundreds of other plant chemicals to be used as a cardiac drug. Critics of herbs and herbalism often single out one constituent to charge that a plant is unsafe for consumption. Comfrey has been deemed "unsafe" by the FDA because it contains potentially carcinogenic alkaloids. These alkaloids are harmful if ingested in large enough quantities, but what the herbalist will argue is that moderation avoids toxicity, and other constituents in the plant will help to buffer the alkaloids. Many of the foods we eat contain naturally occurring compounds that if isolated or taken in concentrated forms will cause toxic reactions in the body. Asparagus from the supermarket, for example, contains potentially carcinogenic alkaloids. So do broccoli and spinach. But you would have to eat a truckload of vegetables over a short period of time to experience any poisoning effect. Coffee contains thirteen or so "toxic" alkaloids. Cherries contain substances that convert to hydrocyanic acid in the body, which can lead to cyanide poisoning, but if you refrain from eating twenty pounds of them, you will not get sick.

Many plants require extra precautions and attention to preparation because of the high concentrations of toxins they contain. My point is, even the delicious and safe watercress can be overindulged.

Other aspects of toxicity characterize each individual body. Some of us have allergies, another situation where the body cannot effectively deal with one or more substances that have been introduced into it. Some of us are more sensitive than others to certain toxins, and some people have medical conditions that prohibit normal metabolic processes.

Commonsense Guidelines

- Be certain of what you are eating or using in or on your body. Be 110 percent positive about the identity of any wild plant (or anything else) before you use it.

- Never ingest or apply anything beyond what is moderately acceptable by your body. Always test new foods in small quantities.

- If you have allergies or any sensitivities, be extra careful.

- Beware of any underlying medical conditions you may have and of medicines you are taking. Be absolutely certain they are compatible with your plans.

- Listen to your body. If you witness anything out of the ordinary, stop whatever you are doing.

Part I

Edible *and* Medicinal Plants

Alder
Alnus species

Birch Family
Betulaceae

Alnus species represent a small group of plants, from shrubs to medium-sized trees. Male and female catkin-type flowers are borne on the same plant. The female flowers stand upright, and the shorter-lived males are long and drooping. Alders are easy to identify by their unique fruits, called strobiles, which look like miniature (¼- to ½-inch) pine cones. The strobiles develop from the catkin-type flowers of the female plant. Green at first, they later turn brown and woody; they may remain attached to the tree or shrub for an entire winter. The leaves of alder are alternate and simple, with serrated edges. The bark ranges from white to dark gray, with some varieties eventually turning reddish brown when mature. White alder (*A. rhombifolia*) and red alder (*A. rubra*) are probably the most widespread tree-size varieties in western North America, with mountain alder (*A. tenuifolia*) and Sitka alder (*A. sinuata*) representing the most common shrub-size alders.

Blooms: April to June.

Habitat and Range: Most members of the *Alnus* genus are partial to streambeds and other consistently moist areas. Various species can be found across most of North America.

Edibility: Although edible and high in protein, alder catkins do not taste very good. As a food source, they are best remembered for survival purposes.

Medicinal Uses: Modern scientific studies have confirmed that red alder (*A. rubra*) stem bark contains two compounds (betulin and lupeol) that may suppress tumor activity. Blackfeet Indians used an infusion of the bark to treat tuberculosis and lymphatic disorders. The leaf tea, used as a skin wash, is said to be a soothing remedy for poison oak, insect bites, and other skin irritations.

Alumroot
Heuchera species

Saxifrage Family
Saxifragaceae

Members of this large genus are typically rock dwellers. Alumroot can often be found growing where soil has collected in the fissures of vertical stone escarpments. A perennial, alumroot is characterized by clusters of leathery, 1- to 3-inch, oval or heart-shaped leaves that grow directly off the root crowns on proportionately long leaf stalks (petioles). The leaves are deeply indented at their bases and look somewhat like those of currant (*Ribes* species). The flowers are small and cup shaped, have five petals, range from light pink to greenish white, and are arranged on leafless stalks that extend well above the rest of the plant, growing to 20 inches. Some species present their flowers along only one side of the stalk. The taproot is proportionately large and covered with a scaly brown skin.

Blooms: April to June.

Habitat and Range: Moist, rocky banks and streambeds across most of North America, from coastal rainforests to alpine meadows above 10,000 feet.

Edibility: All members of the Saxifrage family are edible, at least to a limited degree. The high tannin content of alumroot makes its leaves sour and astringent to the tongue, but small amounts may sharpen the flavor of bland greens.

Medicinal Uses: The root of this plant may contain as much as 20 percent of its weight in tannins, acid compounds that serve to shrink swollen, moist tissues. Alumroot's strong astringency is likely to have earned the plant its common name. Anyone who has tasted the alum used in pickling has experienced the sensation of a shrinking tongue. Dried and powdered alumroot was used by Northwest Indians as a general digestive tonic, and herbalists still use it to stop minor bleeding and reduce inflammation. It was listed in the United States pharmacopoeia for similar purposes until 1882.

Sitka Alder *Alnus sinuata*

Alumroot *Heuchera* species

Amaranth

Amaranthus species

Amaranth Family
Amaranthaceae

The *Amaranthus* genus is large and generally (and accurately) regarded as any number of vacant-lot weeds. Appearance varies between species but most can be identified by the "rough-to-touch," spiny characteristic of the flower clusters, a trait that has gained this aggressive annual plant a nasty reputation with hay farmers. Besides their spiny texture, the tightly arranged flower clusters smell somewhat musty, earning the plant another common name, pigweed. Of the dozens of species that grow throughout North America, redroot amaranth (*A. retroflexus*) is perhaps the most widespread and is certainly the easiest to identify. As its name implies, the lower stem and taproot of this species are red or red striped. Flowers bloom from the stem tips (terminally), often in proportionately long racemes. Redroot amaranth can grow to about 60 inches tall but is generally around 24 inches.

Blooms: Early spring to late summer.

Habitat and Range: Waste areas, pastures, gardens, and virtually anywhere else, from Canada to the tropics.

Edibility: The leaves and stems are tasty in salads or cooked like spinach, especially if gathered young. Some varieties of amaranth have been cultivated and specially developed as a food crop. These varieties typically grow to 6 feet or more and produce large, spired, seed-bearing flower clusters that are harvested and processed as a grain crop. Amaranth grain and greens are highly nutritious. Besides protein, they contain a wide spectrum of minerals and vitamins. Amaranth is grown in many Third World countries as a drought-tolerant ally against hunger.

Medicinal Uses: Many nutritionists and herbalists recognize this plant for its value as a nutritional supplement and nutritive tonic.

American Speedwell

Veronica americana

Figwort Family
Scrophulariaceae

American speedwell *(Veronica americana)* is a rhizomatous perennial that inhabits wet soils. Among herbalists, it is the most widely recognized species of its large genus. This 6- to 36-inch-tall, water-loving plant is characterized by small but conspicuous blue or pinkish blue flowers, each with four uneven petals and two stamens, which are borne on stems arising from the upper leaf axils. The opposite leaves range from lance shaped to broadly oval and have toothed or entire margins. The glabrous (hairless) stems often appear red.

Blooms: May to August.

Habitat and Range: Always standing in or near a clean water source; frequently shares habitat with such plants as watercress, skullcap, or monkeyflower at the edges of mountain streams and in spring seeps. Widespread across most of North America, excluding Mexico.

Edibility: The leaves, stems, and flowers of all species may be used like watercress, in salads, sandwiches, or as a potherb. Flavors range from bland to bitter.

Medicinal Uses: Herbalists use American speedwell primarily as an expectorant tea, which is said to help move bronchial congestion and make coughing more productive. It is also said to have astringent and diuretic qualities.

Look-Alike Plants: American speedwell is often mistaken for skullcap or other members of the Mint family. Mints have square (four-sided) stems, speedwell does not.

Redroot Amaranth, or Pigweed   *Amaranthus retroflexus*

American Speedwell   *Veronica americana*

Arrowleaf Balsamroot
Balsamorrhiza sagittata

Sunflower Family
Compositae

This taprooted perennial displays brilliant yellow, 2- to 4-inch-diameter flowers that immediately bring the Sunflower family to mind. The distinctively arrow-shaped leaves are large (up to a foot long) and grow directly off the root crown on long petioles. The entire plant is covered with tiny hairs that give the leaves a smooth but tacky texture and a silver gray appearance. Although the *Sagittata* species of this genus is the most common and widespread variety, several other species inhabit western North America. All species share a similar appearance.

Blooms: April to July.
Habitat and Range: On dry hillsides and open meadows, from central and eastern California north into Nevada and eastern Washington, Idaho, Montana, and throughout the Rockies.
Edibility: All parts of this plant are edible but not necessarily enjoyable, as the plant contains a bitter, strongly pine-scented sap. Indians dried and ground the large taproot into a starchy flour for consumption when other foods were scarce.
Medicinal Uses: Herbalists sometimes use the root of this plant as an expectorant and mild immunostimulant. Native Americans used the sticky sap as a topical antiseptic for minor wounds.
Look-Alike Plants: This plant is frequently confused with *Wyethia* species (mule's ears), which share the same habitat and flowering characteristics but have sharply lance-shaped leaves that lack the fuzzy silver gray appearance of arrowleaf balsamroot.

Beargrass
Xerophyllum tenax

Lily Family
Liliaceae

This stout perennial first appears as a clump of long (up to 24 inches), wiry, sharply saw-edged, bluish green leaves that bring to mind an exotic ornamental grass. As the plant matures it develops an unbranched central stalk, which produces a showy white terminal raceme of flowers. When the plant first blooms, the raceme is crowded and hemispherical, but as the fruits mature the raceme becomes increasingly elongated. Reproducing mainly off its extensive but shallow rhizomes, a stand of beargrass that appears to be a profusion of individual plants may in fact be the offshoots of only a few. Each of these offshoots may require five years or more to reach maturity, and each will develop only one flower before dying back. Whether or not an individual offshoot blooms during a given year depends on a countless number of environmental variables and delicate balances within the ecosystem. The shallow root systems of beargrass are easily damaged by soil compression, which may compromise the plant's ability to reproduce. For these reasons, beargrass is an excellent indicator of the general health of its habitat. Existing stands of this beautiful plant (and consequently its habitat) are steadily vanishing in the wake of human impact. The leaves are commercially gathered and sold as a filler for floral arrangements.

Blooms: Occasionally; early to late spring.
Habitat and Range: Montane slopes and forests, up to timberline, from Alaska and Canada south to California.
Edibility: Although not a delicacy, the stringy roots can be boiled and eaten. The strong leaves serve as excellent cordage and were frequently used by Indians to make baskets and other implements.
Medicinal Uses: None known.

Arrowleaf Balsamroot *Balsamorrhiza sagittata*

Beargrass *Xerophyllum tenax*

Bee Balm

Monarda fistulosa

Mint Family
Labiatae

Bee balm is a mint that smells like cultivated varieties of oregano (*Origanum* spe-cies). It is often referred to as wild oregano, and aside from bee balm's pointed leaves, *Monarda* species and *Origanum* species look very similar. Bee balm is also known as wild bergamot or Oswego tea. Like other members of the Mint family, bee balm has four-sided (square) stems and opposite leaves; the leaves may have toothed or smooth margins. The tubular flowers range from rose to purple and are arranged in showy, 1- to 3-inch terminal clusters. The plants are free-seeding perennials that typically grow about 1 foot high but may grow to 5 feet if condi-tions allow. *Monarda didyma,* a variety of bee balm that for the most part has escaped cultivation in the western United States, looks similar, except that the entire plant is generally larger and produces flowers in hotter shades of red (more crimson than purple).

Blooms: June to August.

Habitat and Range: Dry to moderately moist meadows, hillsides, and forest clear-ings up to about 5,000 feet elevation, across most of North America.

Edibility: Used in moderation, the leaves of bee balm can be used as a seasoning where oregano is indicated, or in salads. Young leaves and leaf buds are best. Drying removes some of the bitterness from older plants.

Medicinal Uses: Bee balm contains tymol, an antiseptic compound used in some lead-ing brands of mouthwash. Blackfeet Indians recognized the antiseptic action and frequently used the mashed leaves (a poultice) for treatment of various skin infections, and the tea for mouth and throat infections. Winnebago Indians believed that this plant also acted as a general stimulant. Like most mints, bee balm has a long-standing reputa-tion as a carminative herb, one that aids in the expulsion of gas from the intestinal tract.

Bistort

Polygonum bistortoides

Buckwheat Family
Polygonaceae

Polygonum is a large genus of annual and perennial herbs that are characterized by the angular joints of their stems. These joints look as if someone had tied knots in the stem at the base of each alternate leaf, a characteristic that has earned the genus the common (and generic) name knotweed. American bistort (*P. bistortoides*) is a widely distributed species in the West and serves as a good point of reference in the identification of other bistorts. The flowers are presented as dense, 1- to 2-inch terminal plumes of blossoms that first appear on the erect, reddish stems in varying shades of pink. As the season progresses, the flowers fade to white, and eventually to brown in late summer. The lower blossoms of the plumes develop into bulblets, which drop off to reproduce. Plants can grow to 20 inches but seldom exceed 12 inches, particularly at alpine elevations (above 7,500 feet).

Blooms: Early spring to midsummer, depending mainly on elevation.

Habitat and Range: Moist meadows and forest clearings, from montane foothills to above timberline, from Alaska and British Columbia south to the mountains of south-ern California, and east into the Rockies.

Edibility: All members of the *Polygonum* clan are edible, but to varying degrees of palatability. The bistorts are perhaps the best. The roots taste somewhat like chestnuts and can be eaten raw or fire roasted. The seeds, like those of other members of the Buckwheat family, can be ground into flour or roasted whole to thicken stews and make breads.

Medicinal Uses: The roots can be dried, powdered, and used as a simple astringent and styptic agent to relieve minor skin irritations and to stop minor bleeding. Maritime explorers sometimes ate the roots to prevent scurvy. A traditional European "Easter pudding" contains bistort, nettle, and dock, three plant varieties high in vitamin C.

Bee Balm   *Monarda fistulosa*

American Bistort   *Polygonum bistortoides*

Blue Camas
Camassia quamash

Lily Family
Liliaceae

This 8- to 20-inch perennial produces a light blue to deep purple, terminally arranged spike of flowers that stands conspicuously above the surrounding meadow flora. The narrow leaves arise from the base of the plant in a classic lily fashion and may grow as tall as the flower stalk. The individual flowers are star shaped and have yellow anthers (the pollen-bearing part). The bulb is egg shaped with a brown coat.

Blooms: April to June, depending mainly on climate, elevation, and snowpack.

Habitat and Range: Only in meadows that are very moist in the spring but dry out by late summer, from British Columbia south into northern California and east into the mountains of Montana, Wyoming, and northern Utah.

Edibility: The bulb of this plant held great value for many Indian tribes. Several deadly conflicts resulted between tribes over harvest rights, trade discrepancies, and religious issues. The roasted bulbs are sweet, and the plant's common name is derived from the Nootka Indian word *chamas*, which means "sweet."

Look-Alike Plants: Blue camas shares a similar appearance and often the same habitat with its deadly relative, death camas (*Zigadenus elegans*). Fortunately, the two are easily distinguished when in bloom: Death camas has white to cream-colored flowers, but blue camas flowers are always a shade of blue or purple (see death camas).

Medicinal Uses: None known.

Buffalo Berry
Shepherdia canadensis

Oleaster Family
Elaeagnaceae

Buffalo berry is a low, spreading shrub, generally less than 5 feet tall but sometimes growing to 9 feet. It is easily identified by its ½- to 1-inch-long opposite leaves, each with a dark green upper surface and a lighter underside that is covered with tiny but conspicuous brown scales. This gives them a unique, one-sided polka-dot appearance. Buffalo berry produces inconspicuous, yellow green flowers. The fruits are usually on the smaller side of ½ inch, contain one seed, and range from yellow (least common) to bright red (most common). *Shepherdia argentea* (thorny buffalo berry) is a larger species, which bears spines and prefers moister habitats than the more common *S. canadensis*.

Blooms: Midspring to late spring.

Habitat and Range: *Shepherdia canadensis* is common in subalpine forest clearings, where it often serves as an earth regenerator after forest fires or the effects of human impact; extends across northern North America from Oregon to Alaska and east into the New England states. *Shepherdia argentea* is predominantly a riparian shrub, growing sporadically from British Columbia to southern California, and east into Minnesota and central Canada.

Edibility: When you taste the berries of this plant, you briefly experience a pleasant, sweet flavor, which is quickly overcome by a soaplike bitterness. Cooking them with mass quantities of sugar is said to improve the flavor somewhat but not enough to place them on anyone's favorite food list. Like the early Indians, even wildlife reserves them for times when better foods are scarce.

Medicinal Uses: The berries are high in saponin, a slippery, oily compound that gives them their characteristic bad flavor and another common name, soapberry.

Native Americans and early settlers crushed the berries and made a tea for use as a liquid soap; they sometimes drank it to help relieve constipation.

Look-Alike Plants: Buffalo berry is sometimes confused with red root *(Ceanothus velutinus)*, as the plants share the same habitat and similar growth characteristics. Once the two are compared side-by-side, however, differences in the leaves, berries, and bark become obvious.

> **WARNING!** The saponin content of this plant can irritate the stomach if consumed in large quantities.

Blue Camas   *Camassia quamash*   Buffalo Berry   *Shepherdia canadensis*

Bugleweed
Lycopus americanus

Mint Family
Labiatae

Like other mints, bugleweed has four-sided (square) stems, flowers at the upper leaf axils, and opposite leaves. But the unique leaves of *Lycopus americanus*, deeply and irregularly lobed, differentiate it from other mints (and even other species of *Lycopus*). Other species of bugleweed (such as the less common *L. unifloris* and *L. asper*) have leaves not deeply lobed but simple and coarsely toothed, making them difficult to differentiate from other mints, such as skullcap. The easily identified *L. americanus* is by the far the most common and conspicuous variety in North America, making it the bugleweed to remember. Bugleweed, unlike many other mints, does not have a minty odor. Small, whitish to pink flowers are whorled in the leaf axils. The stems may be lightly to moderately hairy, particularly toward the base of the plant.

Blooms: Early to midsummer.
Habitat and Range: Streambanks and marshes, typically found beneath willows and other shrubs. *Lycopus americanus* is widespread across most of North America.
Edibility: Although the raw leaves are edible, they are usually bitter and tough. The wild food forager will likely find more palatable members of the Mint family in close proximity to where he or she finds bugleweed.
Medicinal Uses: Bugleweed preparations are well known from folkloric accounts as effective cough remedies; in fact, this reputation has earned it the common name water horehound, which derives from another long-standing cough medicine favorite, horehound *(Marrubium vulgare)*. Bugleweed is also believed to have diuretic, hemostatic, and mildly sedative effects when used in tea or tincture form.

Bunchberry
Cornus canadensis

Dogwood Family
Cornaceae

An evergreen perennial, bunchberry often stands as the predominant ground cover in heavily timbered areas where low light conditions and high soil acidity may prevent many other plants from growing. It reproduces mainly from its sprawling rhizomes, commonly creating a dense, matted profusion of foliage on an otherwise blank forest floor. The flowers are white, four petaled, and distinctively eye shaped. The leaves are oval but pointed and overlap in three opposite pairs (for a total of six leaves per plant). Like other members of the Dogwood family, each leaf has distinctive parallel veins containing a sticky latex. The latex can be seen as it stretches between two halves of a torn leaf (see red osier dogwood). By midsummer the showy white flowers die back and a "bunch" of bright red berries begins to develop. The entire plant may reach 6 inches high.

Blooms: April to June.
Habitat and Range: Moist, cool, heavily timbered areas, particularly where the forest floor compost is deep and undisturbed; in coniferous forests of North America from Canada south to northern California in the west, and south from Canada into West Virginia in the eastern half of the United States.
Edibility: The ripe berries may be eaten raw or cooked in moderate quantities, but taste rather bland. Excessive consumption will lead to a strong laxative effect.
Medicinal Uses: Cornine and an assortment of various flavonoid compounds have earned this plant a reputation as an anti-inflammatory and general analgesic among contemporary herbalists, and researchers are investigating its properties as an anti-cancer agent. Modern interest in bunchberry's pharmaceutical qualities may have stemmed from its Native American reputation as an antidote to a variety of poisons.

American Bugleweed *Lycopus americanus*

Bunchberry in bloom, *Cornus canadensis.* Inset: Bunchberry with berries

Burdock
Arctium minus

Sunflower Family
Compositae

Burdock is a biennial that grows in its first year as a rosette of large (up to 12 inches long) heart-shaped leaves. During the second year, the plant continues skyward, often reaching 6 to 8 feet while branching out to produce multitudes of thistlelike, light lavender to purple-flowered, seed-bearing burrs at the upper leaf axils and branch ends. Each burr contains several small black seeds and is covered by reverse-hooked spines that enable them to stick to anything that brushes by. The entire plant is covered with tiny hairs, giving the leaves and stems a tacky texture similar to ultrafine sandpaper. The light brown, carrotlike taproot may weigh 2 or 3 pounds and extend 2 or more feet beneath a second-year plant. This sturdy taproot, combined with the annoying and extremely efficient reproductive qualities of the burrs, has earned burdock a reputation as a hated farm and garden enemy.

Blooms: Midsummer to late summer,

Habitat and Range: Rich, deep, consistently moist soil; frequently grows in profuse abundance along the margins of cultivated fields and at roadsides (particularly where human or livestock traffic can cooperate with the hitchhiking burrs). A Eurasian import that has made itself at home across most of North America.

Edibility: Rich in vitamins and iron, burdock was originally brought to North America as a food crop. It is still popular as a market vegetable in much of Europe and Asia. All of the plant is edible. In Eastern Asian cuisine, the roots are often peeled, sliced, and served as a delicious and nutritious stir-fry vegetable or in soups. The stems can be peeled and steamed; the leaves can be boiled and served as you would serve spinach. The key to enjoyment is to collect only the youngest of plants. In North America, organically grown burdock root is beginning to show up in the vegetable coolers of many health food markets.

Medicinal Uses: The medicinal history of burdock may well predate its food use. In Chinese medicine, burdock root has been regarded as an effective "blood purifier" for thousands of years. Today, it is popular and respected among herbal practitioners of all cultures as a safe but powerful liver tonic. Empirical accounts and modern scientific research have confirmed burdock's usefulness in the treatment of water retention, rheumatoid conditions, skin disorders attributable to liver dysfunction, high blood pressure, and as a nutritive.

Look-Alike Plants: Burdock is sometimes confused with cocklebur (*Xanthium strumarium*), which looks very similar. The primary distinguishing feature is the burrs of cocklebur, which are generally smaller than burdock's and contain only two flattened seeds, which have pointed tips. The burrs of burdock, on the other hand, contain several (more than two) small seeds.

Burdock, *Arctium minus,* during the first year's growth.
Inset: The thistlelike flowers of Burdock, *Arctium minus.*

California Poppy
Eschscholzia californica

Poppy Family
Papaveraceae

The California state flower is a colorful perennial, but it grows as an annual in all but the most southern latitudes of North America. Long a garden favorite in much of North America, it has escaped cultivation in many areas, and is often planted along highway margins as a landscape flower. California poppy is easily identified by its showy, four-petaled, sometimes white or yellow but usually bright orange flowers, and by its distinctive leaves and seed capsules. The leaves are like carrot leaves, each one repeatedly and pinnately compounded in groups of three small, narrow segments. The seed capsules are proportionately long and linear, like little green swords.

Blooms: March to June, depending on climatic variations.
Habitat and Range: Wild stands of this sun-loving, drought-tolerant plant can be found from the Columbia River gorge of Washington and Oregon south throughout the coastal and foothill areas of California (where it is illegal to pick it).
Edibility: The flower petals add vibrant color to salads but do not lend enough food value to justify their harvest.
Medicinal Uses: California poppy has the reputation of being a nonaddictive alternative to the opium poppy, but this reputation is unfounded. *Eschscholzia californica* is mildly sedative and analgesic, but its actions are almost nil compared to its narcotic counterpart. In fact, California poppy is cultivated and used by herbal practitioners (especially in England) as a safe and gentle sedative for hyperactive children. American Indians used the plant for similar purposes, and in the treatment of spastic colon and gallbladder conditions. For any devious readers seeking recreational plant exploits, forget it. You won't find any satisfaction in the abuse of this plant.

Cascara Sagrada
Rhamnus purshiana

Buckthorn Family
Rhamnaceae

Cascara sagrada (also known as chittam bark) is a deciduous shrub or small tree characterized by simple, alternate, predominantly veined leaves and small, cup-shaped, greenish yellow flowers. The flowers bloom in umbel-shaped clusters on small but distinctive peduncles (flower stems) borne at the leaf axils. The fruits are presented as dark (nearly black) berries, each containing two or three seeds. Long-term market demand and unethical harvest practices, which denude the plant of its bark, have dramatically reduced the cascara population in many areas.

Blooms: Early to midspring.
Habitat and Range: Most frequently found in densely forested woodlands and on shrub-covered coastal foothills, particularly in moist ravines and along streambanks from British Columbia to southern California, predominantly west of the Cascades and Sierra Nevada, but to a small extent into central Idaho. An eastern variety with the same medicinal properties, *Rhamnus caroliniana*, grows from Virginia into the Carolinas and from Nebraska to Texas.
Edibility: Not edible.
Medicinal Uses: Cascara bark is a well-known laxative that has been widely used by mainstream physicians and in over-the-counter preparations for hundreds of years. It is used in many commercial preparations, with up to three million pounds of the

bark harvested annually. The bark is stripped from the shrub and then must be heat treated, or dried for up to two years, before it can be used for the intended "next morning" results. The fresh, raw bark tends to be strongly cathartic, causing acute and severe diarrhea and vomiting. American Indians sometimes used it in this capacity as an emetic to induce vomiting in cases of poison ingestion.

California Poppy *Eschscholzia californica*

Cascara Sagrada *Rhamnus purshiana*

Catnip

Nepeta cataria

Mint Family
Labiatae

Wild catnip is always a pleasant discovery. Its pungent, tangy-mint aroma wafts to the nose with the slightest disturbance of the plant. The flavor and soothing effects of catnip tea are likely to please even the most discriminating palate. Characteristically a mint, catnip has four-sided (square) stems and opposite leaves. The leaves are petiolate, coarsely but often bluntly toothed, and range from nearly heart shaped to broadly lanceolate. Once you have become familiar with this plant, its aroma is a dead giveaway. The entire plant is distinctively fuzzy, with a texture like flannel. Unlike most other mints, which bloom in whorls at the upper leaf axils (field mint, bugleweed, hedge nettle) or in terminate clusters or spires (bee balm or giant hyssop), catnip blooms both at the upper leaf axils *and* in spikelike terminate clusters. Because catnip frequently grows along irrigation channels and at the edges of cultivated fields, the herbalist or wild food forager often may have difficulty finding uncontaminated plants. Fortunately, catnip is available at many nurseries.

Blooms: Midsummer to late summer.

Habitat and Range: Grows in full sun and rich, moist soils and most frequently found in disturbed areas; a Eurasian import that has become widespread across North America.

Edibility: Young leaves and buds are delicious and nutritious when added in moderation to green salads, particularly with a lemon or herb vinaigrette. The dried leaves and flowers make an excellent tea, high in trace minerals and vitamins. If you enjoy herb teas, I recommend this plant for your garden. Freshly dried, carefully grown catnip is delightfully different from what comes inside a "catnip mouse" from the pet store. Your cat will appreciate the difference too.

Medicinal Uses: The medicinal attributes of catnip are safe and well established. Although you will not find yourself rolling on the floor licking and kicking your teacup, catnip's effect on humans is mildly similar to the effect enjoyed by cats. It is a subtle, gently relaxing sedative when consumed in tea. Like many mints, the tea is also carminative (helps expel excess gas) and is soothing to an upset or generally overworked digestive tract. If you enjoy spicy food, you know what I mean.

Cattail

Typha latifolia

Cattail Family
Typhaceae

Of all the edible plants found in wetlands of the West, common cattail is probably the most widely recognized. It is characterized by its tall stature (up to 9 feet tall), long, narrow leaves, and slender spikelike flower clusters. Lesser cattail *(Typha angustifolia)* is also present in the West and shares the same general appearance and habitat. Its slightly smaller average size and different flower presentation will go unnoticed by all but the discriminating botanist. Both species are equally useful.

Blooms: May to July.

Habitat and Range: Cattails are water plants, often standing as the predominant cover in shallow waters and at the edges of lakes, sloughs, and slow-moving streams across North America.

Edibility: The young shoots can be pulled off the rootstock and peeled in early spring for use as a delicious steamed or stir-fried vegetable. The flavor resembles the bamboo shoots typically used in Chinese cuisine. The young flower heads are excellent when prepared and consumed like corn-on-the-cob, or the pollen can be scraped off, dried, and used as an all-purpose flour. The roots can be peeled and boiled, or dried and made into a flour, although the "pollen flour" is generally favored among wild food connoisseurs. Age and habitat are the primary determining factors in the palatability of this plant. Most people know the flower spikes as smooth, rust-colored "cobs," but the plant is actually past its culinary prime at this stage. The young, green, pollinating flower heads make the best eating. Plants from stagnant or salty water will often taste like a dirty aquarium, and cattails should be avoided altogether if water pollution is suspected.

Medicinal Uses: Although seldom used by modern herbalists, folkloric remedies called for boiling and crushing the roots for use as a poultice for burns and various skin irritations. The flower heads are slightly astringent and were sometimes used by American Indians to relieve diarrhea and other digestive disorders.

Look-Alike Plants: Although the flowering plants are easy to identify, the young shoots closely resemble several unrelated plant species, including toxic members of the Orchid and Lily families. The wild food forager should carefully monitor a specific stand of plants throughout the growth cycle before gathering young shoots the following year.

Catnip *Nepeta cataria*   Common Cattail *Typha latifolia*

Chickweed
Stellaria media

Pink Family
Carophyllaceae

Common chickweed is a weak-stemmed, sprawling annual commonly found in lush, low-growing mats or entangled in other growth (often in the rose bed). Chickweed exhibits a unique characteristic that makes it easy to distinguish from all look-alikes: a line of minute hairs runs up only one side of the stem, switching sides at each pair of leaves. Opposite leaves may grow 1½ inches long and range from broadly lanceolate to ovate, but always with distinct points at their tips. The flowers are small (¼ inch across) and white, with five petals, cleft at the tips, which gives the false appearance of ten petals. The flowers and the small oval seed capsules are suspended away from the main stems of the plant on proportionately long stalks borne from the leaf axils. The reproductive prowess of this plant compensates for its structural frailties, for as the weak stems fall to the ground from the weight of the leaves they take root at their many nodes and extend their outward sprawl. Despite being an annual, chickweed blooms continuously, constantly dropping seeds as it spreads relentlessly.

Blooms: Continuously throughout growth.

Habitat and Range: Moist meadows, ravines, and disturbed areas across all of North America, from the Brooks Range of Alaska to all points south.

Edibility: Chickweed is without doubt one of the most enjoyable wild salad greens in existence. The entire plant is juicy, tender, and mildly sweet throughout its growth, especially where it grows in shade, with a flavor similar to iceberg lettuce. The culinary qualities and easy cultivation of this plant have not been entirely overlooked by the gourmet vegetable industry; chickweed makes occasional appearances on salad menus and at natural food markets.

Medicinal Uses: Chickweed has a long-standing reputation as a safe and reliable emollient, demulcent, refrigerant, and diuretic medicine. Chickweed poultices are often used by herbalists to cool and soothe minor burns and skin irritations, particularly ones associated with itching and dryness. It is an ingredient in many commercial salve and ointment preparations.

Look-Alike Plants: Chickweed is frequently confused with members of the *Cerastium* genus, a group of plants in the same family (Carophyllaceae) that share similar common names (such as field chickweed) and similar appearances. Although generally harmless to the confused forager or herbalist, *Cerastium* lacks the culinary and medicinal appeal of *Stellaria media*. The distinguishing factor is chickweed's one-sided stem hair characteristic. *Cerastium* stems are completely covered with hairs.

Chickweed flowers   *Stellaria media*

Chickweed's unique, single line of stem hairs.   *Stellaria media*

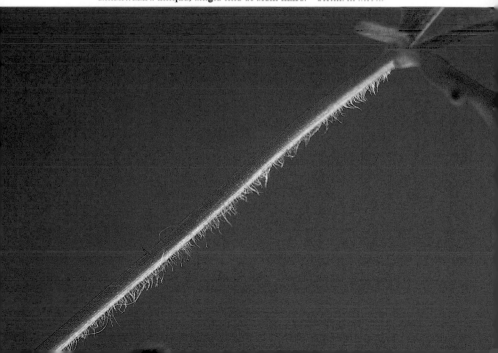

Chicory
Cichorium intybus

Sunflower Family
Compositae

Chicory is a 1- to 6-foot-tall, taprooted perennial with strong, erect stems and spreading branches at its top half. Its growth begins as a basal rosette of rough, lance-shaped, coarsely toothed or sometimes pinnately divided leaves. As the plant reaches skyward and begins branching, the leaves become progressively smaller toward the top, until they become almost inconspicuous in contrast to the showy flowers. The bright blue or occasionally purple (and even less frequently, white) 1- to 1½-inch flowers are the best way to quickly and accurately identify this plant. They are arranged atop or very closely aside the upper branches in the leaf axils, and on close inspection, you can see that each petal is square and distinctly cleft at its tip. The stems will bleed milky juice when damaged.

Blooms: July to September.

Habitat and Range: Common to roadsides and other disturbed areas; not picky about soil but always prefers full sun. Imported from the Mediterranean, chicory is now widespread across most of North America.

Edibility: Chicory was introduced to this continent as a salad green and coffee substitute. The roasted, ground roots were once a popular coffee substitute, particularly when real coffee was either unavailable or too expensive. Although chicory "coffee" is still available in the marketplace as a "healthy, caffeine-free alternative," it has never gained popularity among a growing audience of coffee connoisseurs.

Medicinal Uses: Modern herbalists regard chicory as a weak alternative to dandelion. It has diuretic, laxative, and mild liver-stimulant qualities, and is sometimes used to treat water retention and rheumatoid conditions. Although coffee is more toxic, long-term consumption of chicory may lead to a visual weakness in the retina.

Chiming Bells
Mertensia species

Borage Family
Boraginaceae

Also known as bluebells, mountain bluebells, or oyster leaf, *Mertensia* species represents a fairly large genus of plants, with at least nine species in the Pacific Northwest alone. Although most of these species are frequently referred to as bluebells, this common name is generic, representing dozens of other unrelated plants, such as *Campanula* species, a genus of the Harebell family. For the purpose of breaking a continuum of confusion, I have used the less common name, chiming bells, for this group of plants. The genus is characterized by blue (less frequently pink) trumpet- or bell-shaped flowers that (in most species) dangle as if they were chiming. The lance-shaped leaves are alternate and somewhat succulent in texture, and are often arranged so close together toward the top of the plants that they seem almost opposite one another. The flower petals are united from their bases almost to their tips, giving the flowers a tubular appearance. Species are categorized by size and habitat. Tall species (1 to 5 feet) grow in moist habitats *(M. ciliata, M. paniculata)*, and short species (less than 1 foot) grow in drier subalpine to alpine zones *(M. oblongifolia, M. longiflora, M. bella, M. perplexa)*.

Blooms: Early to midspring.

Habitat and Range: Woodlands, slopes, and burn areas from Alaska into California, east to the eastern slopes of the Rockies.

Edibility: The leaves have a mild but distinct oysterlike flavor. They are an excellent trail snack, but lend themselves best to a good stir-fry dish. Chiming bells may contain alkaloids and other constituents that can be toxic if consumed in large quantities.

Medicinal Uses: None known.

Chicory *Cichorium intybus*

Chiming Bells *Mertensia oblongifolia*

Chokecherry

Prunus virginiana

Rose Family
Rosaceae

Chokecherry is a small tree or shrub (up to 20 feet tall). The leaves are lance to egg shaped, 1 to 4 inches long, may or may not have serrated edges, and are sometimes slightly hairy on their undersides. The small, white to yellowish flowers are presented in narrow, grape-cluster-like inflorescences, which later develop into clusters of red to purple ¼- to ½-inch fruits that resemble miniature cherries. Several other varieties of *Prunus* species grow throughout North America; their physical characteristics and useful traits vary.

Blooms: April to June.

Habitat and Range: Common to streambanks, slopes, and woodlands up to about 5,000 feet, *P. virginiana* ranges from British Columbia east to Newfoundland, and south to North Carolina and Missouri in the East, to New Mexico and California in the West.

Edibility: Chokecherry fruits are usually present from late July into fall, at least so long as the hungry birds, bears, deer, and people leave them alone. They are usually too sour for people to eat raw, but lend themselves well to jelly, wine, or syrup. The stony pits must first be removed before consumption—not only will they break your teeth but, like market-variety cherries, they contain hydrocyanic acid, a compound that can cause nausea and other digestive discomforts if consumed in large enough quantities. Pit removal is as simple as cooking the berries with sugar, then straining the mixture through a sieve to separate the syrup from the pits.

Medicinal Uses: Chokecherry bark used to be a popular cough and chest cold medicine among American Indians and early settlers. In fact, the cherry flavoring many of us remember from the dreaded cough syrups of our youth was probably first inspired from early preparations of chokecherry, as the tasty fruits were often added to make the medicine more palatable. American Indian uses also included preparations of the inner bark in the treatment of diarrhea, sore throats, worms, headaches, and even heart conditions.

Chokecherry fruits   *Prunus virginiana*

Cleavers
Galium aparine

Madder Family
Rubiaceae

The *Galium* genus is large and widespread, with no fewer than thirteen species in the Pacific Northwest alone. Species can be divided into two groups: perennial and annual. The annual varieties are sprawlers and climbers, often forming ground-covering mats, with much weaker taproots and more delicate stems and leaves than perennial species. All *Galium* species have four-sided stems and slender leaves that grow in whorled clusters of two to eight (depending on the species), radiating like the spokes on a wheel. The flowers are very small and white to greenish. *Galium aparine* is a widely distributed annual variety that has earned most of the appeal from the herb market because it is delicate, aromatic, and readily water soluble. It is called cleavers or tangleweed because of the thousands of infinitesimal, reversed hooks on the angles of its stems. These tiny hooks enable the plant to cling to just about anything in a fashion similar to the way static-charged hair will cling to clothing. This allows cleavers to reproduce effectively, as the delicate, seed-bearing foliage is easily uprooted and carried away by a passerby. Perennial varieties such as northern bedstraw *(G. boreale)* do not share this unique characteristic.

Blooms: May to July.

Habitat and Range: *Galium aparine* (cleavers) and most other annual varieties prefer moist habitats and commonly grow in shaded ravines and along streams. *Galium boreale* (northern bedstraw) and other perennial species can tolerate a wider diversity of habitats and commonly inhabit road margins and dry, sunny areas. Cleavers and northern bedstraw are common across North America and most of the Northern Hemisphere, up to about 6,000 feet.

Edibility: All *Galium* species smell and taste sweet. The leaves and foliage were once used as a fragrant mattress and pillow stuffing, hence the common name bedstraw. Although the young leaves lend themselves well to salads, the wild foods forager should bear in mind that the stems of clinging varieties *(G. aparine)* do not discriminate between your clothing and the back of your throat. I learned this the hard (and embarrassing) way, during an edible plant demonstration that resulted in a gagging fit. The hookless perennial varieties, although less tender and juicy, are much more enjoyable. All varieties make a pleasant, palatable tea.

Medicinal Uses: "Cleavers herb" is highly regarded among modern herbalists as an effective lymphatic tonic and reliable diuretic medicine. Taken internally, the fresh plant tea is believed to help stimulate the drainage of lymph-engorged tissues. The fresh plant juice is also reputed to help cool and soothe minor burns and skin irritations.

Northern Bedstraw *Galium boreale*

Cleavers *Galium aparine*

Coltsfoot

Petasites species

Sunflower Family

Compositae

Coltsfoot is a perennial that produces its flowers on a leafless stem before the leaves fully develop. The flowers are generally drab and featherlike, ranging in color from white to light purple, and developing in terminal clusters atop a reddish stem. The leaves vary in shape according to species, from triangular *(Petasites frigidus* var. *nivalis)* or narrowly arrow shaped *(P. sagittata)* to broadly oval shaped with deep, palmate lobes *(P. palmatus)*. The 3- to 10-inch-wide leaves are presented on long petioles that extend directly from thick, creeping rootstocks. The leaves are dark green on the upper surfaces and lighter and feltlike on the undersides.

Blooms: Late March to early June.

Habitat and Range: Requires consistent moisture at its feet and usually grows along streams, in wet meadows, and on shaded road margins, particularly where water continuously seeps. Several species range in forested areas from Alaska south to California, and east across the northern half of North America.

Edibility: The flowering stem may be boiled as a potherb or stir-fried. Leaves may be cooked like spinach, but tend to be too feltlike in texture for enjoyment by most palates. The entire aboveground plant has a mild but distinctive saltiness, a trait that prompted its early use as a salt substitute.

Medicinal Uses: Coltsfoot has a time-honored tradition among herbalists as an expectorant and cough suppressant. It has been used for hundreds of years in the treatment of respiratory ailments ranging from chest colds to whooping cough, asthma, and viral pneumonia. Externally, a decoction of the herb is said to be effective in the symptomatic treatment of arthritis. In Europe, the dried leaves are smoked as a popular treatment for chronic coughs, the theory being that the plant has constituents that act as antihistamines and may also work to impede the nerve impulses that trigger coughing.

> **WARNING! Coltsfoot contains a group of alkaloids that may be harmful if consumed in large quantities.**

Coltsfoot   *Petasites palmatus*

Coptis
Coptis species

Buttercup Family
Ranunculaceae

Coptis inhabits dark, dense, pristine forest habitats. It is naturally suited to low light conditions and cannot survive full sun. These requirements, compounded by the continued loss of the necessary habitat and a growing scientific and economic interest in the plant, have brought the future of coptis into question. Coptis is an important ally to humanity and to the environment it serves, and to assure its survival means to set aside greed and recognize not only its worth to us but the purpose it serves within its ecosystem. First, we must recognize the plant.

Coptis is a rhizomatous perennial that sprawls across the forest floor by its extensive horizontal root system. The long and threadlike roots play a critical role in breaking up the continuity of the thick forest compost that might otherwise be impervious to water, air, and other elements essential to the survival of the forest floor community. If you scratch the outer surface of the root, you will see the bright, goldenrod yellow inner tissues, a characteristic that has earned coptis the common name goldthread. The stems of coptis are strong and wiry. The ¾- to 1½-inch leaves are on proportionately long petioles, have surfaces that are shiny and plasticlike in texture, and are compounded into groups of three leaflets, each one deeply lobed or pinnately divided into two or three parts. The flowers are distinctive and unusual, with inconspicuous petals but five to eight sepals that give them the appearance of ½- to 1-inch-wide starbursts. The entire plant is seldom more than 10 inches high.

Blooms: May to July.

Habitat and Range: Shaded coniferous forests, particularly where cedars are present, from Alaska south to the mountains of central California and east into the Rocky Mountains of Montana and Idaho. The range of *Coptis triflora* (three-leafed goldthread) extends into Siberia and Japan. *Coptis groenlandica* is present in the eastern half of North America, from Canada to North Carolina.

Edibility: Not edible.

Medicinal Uses: Coptis has a time-honored reputation as a strong antimicrobial medicine and was in widespread use in America up until about 1930. Back then, the root was commonly used to treat open sores of the mouth, hence another of its common names, cankerroot. The alkaloid constituents in coptis root closely parallel those of the popular herb goldenseal in their medicinal actions. In recent studies of Chinese medicines, *C. sinensis* was shown to be active against HIV, hepatitis B, and several forms of influenza (at least in the laboratory). This plant offers many great hopes to humanity, but the stage is set for the same disproportionate marketplace sensationalism that has all but wiped out wild stands of another promising ally, goldenseal. Coptis faces the loss of its pristine home. It is up to us to recognize and change this trend.

Coptis *Coptis occidentalis*

Cow Parsnip
Heracleum lanatum

Parsley Family
Umbelliferae

Cow parsnip is unquestionably the easiest member of the Umbel family to recognize. Like other members of the carrot-parsley clan, *Heracleum* has umbrella-shaped clusters of tiny white flowers borne atop hollow stems. But this is where most of the similarities with the other umbels, including the deadly water hemlock, end. The large (up to 12 inches wide), deeply lobed, sometimes hairy leaves distinguish cow parsnip. The entire plant, particularly the large, light brown, tapered taproot, smells somewhat rank. The seeds are also distinctive—essentially flat, ¼ to ½ inch wide, papery in texture, and each exhibiting four distinct black lines on only one of their surfaces. Cow parsnip is the largest member of its family in North America, with mature plants averaging 2 to 6 feet tall in the lower forty-eight states and as much as 10 feet tall in Alaska and at other latitudes where long days encourage rapid growth.

Blooms: May to August.

Habitat and Range: Moist meadows and riparian habitats from Alaska to California and east throughout the Rocky Mountains.

Edibility: Cow parsnip roots are edible but tend to be overly strong and bitter. The young leaves are better, but not necessarily tasty, when cooked.

Medicinal Uses: Cow parsnip root or seeds are sometimes used by herbalists as a digestive antispasmodic and to remedy diarrhea. The mature, green seeds have a mild anesthetic action on the tissues of the mouth; when gently chewed and sucked, they will numb the tongue and gums in a manner similar to clove oil. In the mid-1800s, a decoction of the root was believed to be a cure for epilepsy.

> **WARNING! Although uncommon, documented cases of contact dermatitis have developed after handling cow parsnip.**

Cranesbill Geranium
Geranium viscosissimum

Geranium Family
Geraniaceae

Also known as sticky wild geranium because of the texture of its foliage, cranesbill geranium is commonly seen as the predominant summer show of bright pink in grasslands of the Mountain West. The entire plant is sticky-hairy, growing as high as 32 inches, with palmate leaves that extend directly from the base of the plant and may reach 12 inches long. The showy, five-petaled, light pink to purplish red flowers have distinctive hairs on their inner surfaces, and the sepals and flower stalks are covered with yellow-tipped hairs. The plant received its common name in recognition of its long, beaklike fruit capsule, a characteristic universal throughout the Geranium family (see filaree).

Blooms: June to August.

Habitat and Range: Grows most commonly in open grasslands but found to a lesser degree in moist areas as well, all the way up to timberline. Generally east of the Cascades, from British Columbia south to northern California and east into Saskatchewan and the Rocky Mountain States.

Edibility: The flowers and leaves are edible, but their astringency and texture is unappealing.

Medicinal Uses: The leaves can be made into a poultice or infused and applied as a safe, topical field remedy for insect bites, rashes, and other minor irritations. Herbalists recognize geranium's value as a gentle remedy for diarrhea and gastric or urinary irritations. The powdered root possesses the strongest astringent action of the plant and was frequently used by Blackfeet Indians to stop bleeding.

Cow Parnsip *Heracleum lanatum*

Cranesbill, or Sticky Wild Geranium *Geranium viscosissimum*

Creosote Bush or Chaparral

Caltrop Family

Larrea tridentata
Zygophyllaceae

Although this book focuses primarily on plants in the Mountain and Pacific West, it would be incomplete without examining this historically rich but presently controversial desert dweller. Creosote bush, known in the herbal world as chaparral, is the predominant low-desert shrub of the United States Southwest. The abundance of this shrub almost makes a description of it unnecessary, as many people who live or travel between the Pacific and inland states of the Southwest invariably find themselves in what seems to be an endless expanse of these ancient plants. For readers unfamiliar with it, here are the details: creosote bush is the chest-high to 10-foot-tall dark green stuff with spindly, wind-whipped branches that contributes to the highway hypnosis along the road to Las Vegas. The leaves are tiny (⅛ inch) and have a greasy-leathery texture. The bark is reddish brown toward the base of the plant and progressively lighter (to almost white) on the smaller limbs. The flowers are minute and yellow; they eventually develop into oddly fuzzy, seed-bearing capsules. If you traverse the Ocean of Chaparral, get used to it: this is one of the oldest living inhabitants of our planet. Some plants have been carbon dated at more than 10,000 years old.

Blooms: Often blooms after precipitation, usually anytime from March through May.

Habitat and Range: Profusely abundant from the deserts of central Texas west through the southern half of New Mexico and Arizona to the deserts of southern California and Nevada.

Edibility: Not edible.

Medicinal Uses: Anything as old and abundant as creosote bush must be here for a reason. American Indians of the Southwest have used this plant for centuries for everything from the treatment of tumors and hepatic diseases to topical skin treatments, including sunscreen. Today, herbalists use the plant as a strong bacteriostatic and antioxidant agent in the treatment of blood and liver disorders. Recent scientific research and documented incidents, however, have raised new hopes and new concerns. Some studies have shown that chemical constituents in creosote bush may inhibit the growth of cancerous cells, but other studies have shown exactly the opposite. A few recent accounts of serious liver damage have been attributed to this herb. Many theories have emerged about why this plant may suddenly be harming people after thousands of years of safe medicinal use. Perhaps the human body and creosote bush are evolving away from one another. Thousands of people still use the herb chaparral on a daily basis, though, and it is a popular herbal medicine in natural products markets worldwide.

> **WARNING! Recent cases of liver damage have been attributed to the internal use of chaparral or creosote bush (*Larrea tridentata*). The FDA strongly discourages its use.**

Creosote Bush, or Chaparral, in its desert habitat. *Larrea tridentata*

Creosote Bush fruits *Larrea tridentata*

Currant

Ribes species

Gooseberry Family
Grossulariaceae

The *Ribes* genus is quite large and varied, with no fewer than thirty-three species inhabiting the western half of North America. The foremost characteristics to remember in identifying a plant as a member of the currant-gooseberry genus rest in the leaves, the flowers, and the fruits. The alternate leaves are lobed three to seven times at their margins, generally rounded overall, and have palmately arranged veins. The flowers are variable in color, may be solitary or clustered, and have five petals that are smaller than the sepals, each subtended by a bract. The fruits are round, several seeded, and waxy, ranging from yellow to black (with red and purple in between), and usually have the dried remains of the flower still attached. People who have familiarized themselves with this clan of plants by a hands-on, rather than taxonomic, process have learned to differentiate species in a way that is more sensual than scientific. The ones with spines are gooseberries, the ones without are currants, and the ones that taste terrible or delicious are quickly remembered. Golden currant *(Ribes aureum)*, which is named for its flower, not its red fruit, is perhaps the best known of all species. It is spineless, widespread, and very palatable.

Blooms: May to July.

Habitat and Range: Habitat varies greatly between species, but rockslides and riparian habitats from valley elevations to about 6,000 feet are good places to look for the greatest diversity of species in the West. Golden currant, introduced into many areas for its fruit and ornamental value, is a valley floor, riparian habitat variety widespread across North America.

Edibility: Bad news—only a few species of currant are palatable. Those that are (such as golden currant) are slightly sweet and somewhat mealy. Cooked and strained, the fruits make an excellent jelly. To determine palatability before oral involvement, try smelling the fruits; many of them have an unpleasant odor with a flavor to match. If this test fails, do not be alarmed—the entire genus is nontoxic.

Medicinal Uses: American Indians used currant in a wide array of medicinal applications. Blackfeet Indians made a preparation of black currant *(R. hudsonianum)* root for the treatment of kidney and uterine disorders. Cree Indians used the fruits of *R. glandulosum* with the belief that they could help a woman become pregnant. Contemporary herbalists and nutritionists have recognized that the oil of black currant seeds is high in gamma-linolenic acid (GLA), a compound that has proved useful in the treatment of premenstrual syndrome, alcoholism, diabetes, arthritis, metabolic dysfunctions, and eczema (see evening primrose).

Golden Currant fruit *Ribes aureum*

Dandelion

Taraxacum officinale

Sunflower Family
Compositae

Dandelion is probably the most widely recognized and aggressively hated weed in North America. Characterized by its bright yellow flowers, deeply lobed leaves, and its long, stubborn perennial taproots that mark the beginning of another arduous season of yard work, the dandelion has established itself everywhere as an enemy. In fact, many of the weeds we pull from the garden as "dandelions" are not dandelions at all. Several members of the Sunflower family are commonly mistaken for dandelions, and often these look-alikes are consumed by herbalists and foragers who have not followed two simple rules of identification: (1) dandelion has no central stalk and presents no branching characteristics; instead, the leaves of dandelion grow directly off the root crown in a rosette configuration; (2) the leaf surfaces of dandelion are not spiny or fuzzy.

Blooms: Early spring to late summer, depending on climate and ecological niche.

Habitat and Range: Widespread across North America.

Edibility: Dandelion was introduced into North America by European settlers as a food crop and medicinal cure-all. Today, it is still widely marketed as a potherb and salad vegetable throughout Europe, and commercially grown dandelion greens are now gaining popularity in the United States organic foods industry. Picked when young, wild dandelion greens are delicious in salads or prepared like spinach. Older plants become bitter, but much of the bitterness can be alleviated by "blanching" the entire plant under a piece of paper for two weeks or more before harvest. The roots can be roasted and ground for use as a coffee substitute—a poor substitute, in my opinion. Dandelion is rich in vitamins A, C, E, and B-complex. It also contains considerable amounts of iron, protein, and a wide spectrum of trace minerals.

Medicinal Uses: Dandelion has a well-established history as a medicine. Its reputation began in America after it was intentionally imported on the *Mayflower*. Dandelion has been used to cure virtually everything that ails humanity. Its most enduring and documented medicinal attribute is the strong but unique diuretic qualities of the leaves and root; dandelion stimulates urination but also helps in replacing much of the potassium and other trace minerals that are usually lost during diuresis.

Look-Alike Plants: Although generally not toxic, many plants can be mistaken for dandelion. Several species of sowthistle (*Sonchus* species) look similar when young but quickly begin branching out as they grow. Spotted cat's ear (*Hypochaeris radicata*) is similar but has rough-hairy leaves when young. Wild lettuces (*Lactuca* species) also look similar when young, but either have conspicuous spines on their leaves (see prickly lettuce) or develop a central stalk and branching characteristics. Remember—dandelions have no branches!

Dandelion *Taraxacum officinale*

Sowthistle, *Sonchus* species. Note the branching stems; this is *not* a dandelion.

Devil's Club
Oplopanax horridum

Ginseng Family
Araliaceae

Devil's club has rightly earned both its common and Latin species name *(horridum)* by its profusely abundant armament. The entire plant is covered with brittle, sharp yellow spines that have a nasty characteristic of breaking off in the flesh of foraging herbalists and passing hikers. The stems and stalks are covered with these weapons—even the leaf veins are lined with them. The entire plant is well described as primordial in appearance, with large (up to 1 foot wide) maplelike leaves and woody, spine-covered stems that often curve and turn in several directions. The flowers are small and white, borne in terminate, umbrella-shaped inflorescences that later develop into long clusters of bright red berries. The plants can grow quite large, especially in areas of high precipitation. In the rainforests of south Alaska and the Olympic Peninsula of Washington, you can expect to see devil's club more than 8 feet tall.

Blooms: April to June.

Habitat and Range: Moist, dense woods; most abundant in old-growth conifer forests, from south-central Alaska south along the coast into the coastal mountains of California and east into portions of the Idaho Panhandle and northwest Montana.

Edibility: The very, *very,* young shoots are good raw or cooked, but bear in mind that they arm themselves early in life. If the spines are soft and harmless, they are edible.

Medicinal Uses: Because this is a member of the Ginseng family, many herbalists believe that devil's club is a substitute for American ginseng *(Panax quinquefolius)*, an herb that has been sensationalized to near extinction by its reputation as a "mind-enhancer." This belief is a disservice to devil's club, which grows in a habitat sensitive to human impact. Although devil's club shares some pharmacological and therapeutic similarities with ginseng, it is not the same medicine. Contemporary herbalists who can look beyond market sensationalism to the true attributes of devil's club recognize it as a strong respiratory stimulant and expectorant. Its use by Native Americans as a treatment for adult-onset diabetes has been substantiated by scientific studies in this century. Indians also used it to treat cancer.

Devil's Club (young)   *Oplopanax horridum*   Devil's Club (mature)   *Oplopanax horridum*

Devil's Club leaf spines   *Oplopanax horridum*

Echinacea
Echinacea species

Sunflower Family
Compositae

Echinacea, also known as purple coneflower, is a taprooted perennial that may grow as tall as 40 inches. Nine species of *Echinacea* are native to North America, all with flowers in distinctive, conelike central disks. The rays of most species droop away from the disk when mature, with the most common species ranging in color from pale to dark purple. Each ray has a distinctive cleft at its tip. Most species have stiff hairs on the stems and leaves. The leaves are alternate, have distinct lengthwise veins, and may or may not have toothed margins. The leaves range from oval to the more common lance shape, and the ones at the base of the plant grow from proportionately long petioles (leaf stems). The petioles and leaves become progressively shorter and smaller toward the top of the plant. *Echinacea purpurea* is by far the most widely distributed species in North America. For several decades, this species has been popular as a medicinal herb and garden flower. Dozens of cultivars of *E. purpurea* have been developed; nearly the entire world market supply of this species comes from cultivated plants. Several other species, however, such as *E. angustifolia* and *E. pallida,* are quickly succumbing to commercial and environmental pressures. Market pressures and continuing loss of habitat have eliminated most wild stands of echinacea. Its range continues to shrink, and today only small, isolated populations of wild echinacea survive west of the Missouri River.

Blooms: June to August (depending mainly on climate).

Habitat and Range: Mainly an introduced plant in the West, partial to open plains and woodlands. Its natural range once extended from eastern Canada south into the Ozarks and west through the Corn Belt states to the eastern slopes of the Rockies.

Edibility: The colorful flower petals can be used to decorate salads, but otherwise *Echinacea* is not a food plant.

Medicinal Uses: It all started with the American Indians, who used echinacea to treat snakebite and a wide variety of infections. When European settlers discovered the plant, word about its effectiveness quickly spread across the Atlantic, and by the nineteenth century echinacea had become the most popular medicine derived from a North American native plant. Today, it represents a global, multimillion-dollar industry. Echinacea is regarded as the foremost immunostimulant herb, a reputation that is currently being fueled by recognition that perhaps the human autoimmune system has been compromised by the effects of our environment and generations of chemical interference and abuse. Several studies have confirmed the effectiveness of this herb as a preventative tonic that builds the body's defenses against bacterial, viral, or fungal infection. Market sensationalism has exaggerated the usefulness of echinacea out of proportion, with the result that remaining wild stands of it are dramatically and needlessly disappearing under growing market pressures. Echinacea is not a *cure* for anything, but a *preventative* — an immune system booster that may help the body's resistance at early stages of infection. If you use echinacea, please use only products that are labeled as "certified organically grown."

Echinacea *Echinacea purpurea*

Elderberry
Sambucus species

Honeysuckle Family
Caprifoliaceae

Elderberry is a shrub or small tree, usually less than 25 feet high. Its flowers are presented in dense, flat-topped, umbel-like clusters of small, cream-colored blossoms. These clusters may have a span more than 6 inches in diameter and will develop into bunches of powdery blue or bright red ¼-inch berries. The limbs usually droop under the weight of the ripe berries. The leaves are 5 to 9 inches long and are pinnately divided into five to nine serrated leaflets, each with a pointed tip.

Blooms: April to June. Fruits in mid- to late summer.

Habitat and Range: Common to riparian habitats, roadbanks, and moist forest clearings up to timberline. Three blue-fruited species of elderberry inhabit the West, all similar in appearance: *Sambucus cerulea* and *S. racemosa* range from British Columbia to California, Arizona, and throughout the Rocky Mountains; *S. mexicana* (Mexican elder) ranges from northern California south into Mexico and east into Nevada and southwestern New Mexico. One red-fruited species, *S. callicarpa* (Pacific red elder) grows in coastal habitats from southern Alaska to central California; it is considered generally toxic.

Edibility: The berries of all blue varieties are edible. They make excellent jams, jellies, pies, or wine, but beware—the seeds contain hydrocyanic acid, a compound that can lead to nausea and diarrhea if consumed in large enough quantities. This can be avoided by straining out the seeds or thoroughly cooking the berries. Red elderberries contain much higher concentrations of these compounds, and therefore should be regarded as toxic. The flower clusters are nontoxic and delicious when dipped in batter and fried as elder-flower fritters.

Medicinal Uses: American Indians used the inner bark of elder to induce vomiting. In smaller quantities, the bark was used as a diuretic. The decocted inner bark was also used topically as a skin wash for eczema, ulcers, and chronic forms of dermatitis. Contemporary herbalists sometimes use the berries (or rarely, a weak infusion of the inner bark) as a laxative or diaphoretic medicine (that is, to induce sweating). Recent studies have confirmed that the berries possess antiviral properties that may be useful against influenza.

> **WARNING!** Elderberry contains hydrocyanic acid, a compound that may lead to mild cyanide poisoning if consumed in large quantities. The leaves and bark contain the highest concentrations and should not be ingested. Red varieties of elderberry are far more toxic than blue. If the berries are red, do not eat them.

Blue Elderberry fruits and leaves   *Sambucus cerulea*

Blue Elderberry flowers   *Sambucus cerulea*

Evening Primrose
Oenothera species

Evening Primrose Family
Onagraceae

The *Oenothera* genus is large and varied, with more than twenty species inhabiting the West; many species are cultivated for ornamental purposes. The plants may be annual, biennial, or perennial. They all have basally clustered or alternating leaves, which range in appearance from narrowly lance shaped *(O. subacaulis)* to pinnately divided *(O. tanacetifolia)*. The flowers, often fragrant and varying between white, yellow, and occasionally pink, display the most distinctive characteristics of the genus: four petals; four sepals; and eight stamens (the structures that comprise the center of the flower), each holding a globe-shaped or deeply four-lobed stigma (the pollen-bearing part). Fruits are presented as four-celled capsules. As the common name evening primrose implies, the flowers of many species open only at night, closing tightly during daylight hours.

Blooms: April to June.

Habitat and Range: Dry land for the most part, but the range of habitat is variable. Where evening primrose does not grow wild, it can be found in gardens or where it has escaped from cultivation. It grows throughout North America.

Edibility: The roots may be cooked and eaten as a vegetable. They are best when young, becoming tough but somewhat spicy with age (like many of us).

Medicinal Uses: The leaves and stems of evening primrose have an astringent, mucilaginous quality that makes it a useful tea for sore throats and raspy coughs. It is also said to be helpful in treating gastric irritations and, when applied topically (as a poultice), for reducing swelling. The most important and validated medicinal attribute of evening primrose is found in the oils of the seeds: high levels of gamma-linolenic acid (GLA). As a result of more than two hundred studies conducted since 1970, the effectiveness of evening primrose–derived GLA has been attributed to a regulatory effect on systemic fatty acid imbalances and metabolic functions of the liver. In clinical studies it has proved useful in the treatment of heart and vascular diseases, asthma, arthritis, and premenstrual syndrome. Evening primrose oil (in gelcaps) is becoming immensely popular in the natural supplements marketplace (see currant).

Common Evening Primrose (a garden variety)   *Oenothera biennis*

False Solomon's Seal
Smilacina species

Lily Family
Liliaceae

False Solomon's seal is a perennial with long, creeping rootstocks from which solitary, branchless stems emerge in early spring. The leaves are alternate and lance shaped, with the base of each leaf partially clasping the stem (if the leaves clasp completely around the stem, it is not false Solomon's seal). Only two species of *Smilacina* inhabit the West, and they both have small, white, starlike flowers that appear at the tip of the stem. *Smilacina racemosa* is the larger (up to 32 inches tall); it has broader, 2- to 5-inch-long, prominently veined leaves, and has many flowers arranged in a densely clustered raceme. *Smilacina stellata* has narrower, shorter (2- to 3-inch) leaves, and the entire plant is smaller overall (up to 24 inches tall), with only a few flowers presented in a zigzag inflorescence. Both species produce reddish berries after blooming.

Blooms: April to June.

Habitat and Range: Grows in a wide variety of montane habitats up to about 7,000 feet, but the healthiest stands are almost always in partial shade and soft soils. Both species range through mountain forests across North America.

Edibility: The entire plant is edible but tends to be too fibrous and bitter to enjoy. Ojibwa Indians ate the rootstocks after "cooking" them overnight in lye to remove the bitterness. The young shoots are said to be tasty, but they can be difficult to identify positively (see Look-Alike Plants). If you choose to eat this plant, do so in moderation—large quantities of it tend to have strong laxative effects.

Medicinal Uses: Aside from its laxative qualities, false Solomon's seal root is recognized by herbalists as a cough suppressant and respiratory demulcent. American Indians often used a poultice made from the root to treat inflammations of the skin, to relieve sunburn pain, and to stop bleeding. Some Indian tribes even promoted smoking of the roots to "cure insanity" and to quiet emotional children.

Look-Alike Plants: At early stages of growth, false Solomon's seal resembles several other members of the Lily family, some of which are quite toxic (see false hellebore). It is also frequently confused with *Streptopus amplexifolius* (see twisted-stalk). The flowers of this larger, edible relative are presented from the leaf axils, unlike false Solomon's seal's terminate clusters.

False Solomon's Seal   *Smilacina racemosa*

False Solomon's Seal   *Smilacina stellata*

Field Mint
Mentha arvensis

Mint Family
Labiatae

Field mint looks, tastes, and smells like its cultivated relative, peppermint *(Mentha piperita)*. The most pronounced difference between the two are the flowers; peppermint blooms in terminal spikes, and field mint blooms in whorls at the upper leaf axils. Like all mints, the leaves are opposite and the stems are four-sided (square). The leaves are serrated and lance shaped to elliptical. Field mint may reach as high as 20 inches but is usually found on the shorter side of 12 inches. And perhaps the most distinguishing characteristic of all—field mint smells deliciously minty. Besides peppermint *(M. piperita)* that has escaped cultivation, at least five other species of *Mentha* inhabit western North America. All of them have axillary flowers (unlike field mint) and share the typical stem and leaf characteristics of the Mint family. All are edible and medicinally useful but vary in odor and flavor.

Blooms: July to September.
Habitat and Range: Moist soils, especially along streams, up to timberline; throughout the Northern Hemisphere.
Edibility: The leaves may be eaten fresh or dried for a pleasant tea, exactly like peppermint.
Medicinal Uses: The active ingredient is menthol, and like peppermint, field mint has an old and well-validated reputation as an upset stomach remedy, acting as a carminative and as a digestive system antispasmodic (this is where the idea of an "after-dinner mint" came from). Ojibwa Indians also used it as a "blood purifier" and to help reduce fevers.

Filaree
Erodium cicutarium

Geranium Family
Geraniaceae

Also known as storksbill because of its long, five-lobed, beaklike fruits, filaree is commonly recognized as a "lawn and garden weed" throughout North America and most of the world. The pink, five-petaled flowers are usually borne in two or more clusters. The leaves are divided into proportionately narrow, feathery segments. The stems are red and grow from a flattened basal rosette. At northern latitudes, filaree usually grows as a small, ground-hugging annual, often going unnoticed beneath a mat of other "weeds." In warm, precipitous southern regions of North America, filaree may grow as an erect biennial, producing much larger leaves, flowers, and fruits.

Blooms: March to August.
Habitat and Range: Originally introduced from Europe or Asia as a forage crop, now common to gardens, lawns, pastures, and other disturbed areas across North America.
Edibility: The leaves are edible and quite palatable, particularly if picked young, with a sharp parsleylike flavor that complements an otherwise bland tossed green salad.
Medicinal Uses: Although never considered a strong medicine, filaree has a long-standing reputation as a diuretic, astringent, and anti-inflammatory herb. It has been used in Mexico for centuries to control afterbirth hemorrhage and to prevent postpartum infections. In Chinese medicine, the tea is used as a kidney tonic (primarily for kidney trauma) and to control urinary tract bleeding.

Field Mint *Mentha arvensis*

Filaree *Erodium cicutarium*

Fireweed
Epilobium angustifolium

Evening Primrose Family
Onagraceae

Fireweed is well known for its spires of brilliant pink flowers that lend bold contrast to burns and other disturbed areas throughout most of North America. Individual flowers are four petaled and grow in clusters atop erect stems. Alternate leaves are narrowly lance shaped, 4 to 6 inches long, and are paler on the undersides than on top. The leaves bear a resemblance to many species of the unrelated Willow family, a characteristic that has earned fireweed another common name, willow herb. The fruits are presented as slender pods, 1 to 3 inches long, which stand rigidly off the stem. These skinny pods eventually split open to release airborne, seed-bearing cottony puffs. The most distinctive identifying feature of this plant is a unique leaf characteristic. Unlike other plants, the leaf veins do not terminate at the edges of the leaves, but instead join together in loops inside the outer margins. This makes the plant easy to identify throughout all stages of its growth. Two species of this plant predominate in western North America *(Epilobium angustifolium* and *E. latifolia);* they are similar in appearance and share the same range and habitat.

Blooms: April to July.

Habitat and Range: The edges of burns, clearcuts, and other disturbed areas throughout the northern half of North America, where it serves a critical role as an "earth-regenerator," providing a damaged ecosystem with erosion control and a new source of food and habitat.

Edibility: The young leaves and shoots of this plant contain considerable amounts of vitamin C and beta-carotene and are quite palatable, either raw or cooked like spinach. At the early stages of growth, when young leaves are pointed upward along the stems, the entire plant can be snapped off at ground-level and enjoyed like young asparagus. Mature plants tend to become tough and bitter.

Medicinal Uses: If consumed in very large quantities or in the form of a very strong tea, fireweed is a gentle but effective laxative. Early and modern folkloric uses include leaf or flower tea as an antispasmodic remedy in the treatment of whooping cough and asthma. Blackfeet Indians used the root as an astringent and antiseptic poultice in the treatment of minor cuts, abrasions, burns, and other skin irritations. The flowers were rubbed into rawhide to repel water. Modern herbalists find it useful in the treatment of candidiasis.

Look-Alike Plants: At first glance, young fireweed resembles a wide variety of unrelated plant species. Close inspection of its unique leaf vein characteristic, however, confirms identification. After blooming, identification becomes obvious.

Fireweed   *Epilobium angustifolium*

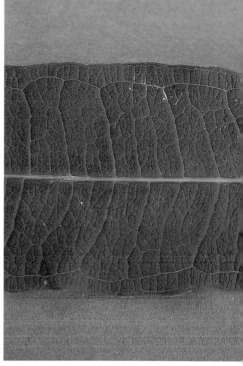

Fireweed leaf veins   *Epilobium angustifolium*

Fireweed (young and tender)   *Epilobium angustifolium*

Glacier Lily
Erythronium grandiflorum

Lily Family
Liliaceae

Also known as fawn lily, trout lily, adder's tongue, or dogtooth violet, *Erythronium* species represent a group of showy perennials that bloom frequently in spectacular abundance, at the margins of melting snowfields. This genus is characterized by its broad pair of basal leaves and the pair of nodding flowers borne atop leafless central flower stalks (peduncles). The flowers are generally on the smaller side of 3 inches in diameter, have six lance-shaped petals and six stamens, and range from white with a yellow band at the base *(E. montanum)* or solid yellow *(E. grandiflorum)* to deep pink *(E. revolutum)*.

Blooms: April to June.

Habitat and Range: Moist woods and meadows, from about 2,500 feet *(E. oregonum)* to above timberline; British Columbia to northern Oregon, and east to the mountains of Idaho, Montana, and Colorado.

Edibility: The leaves and fresh seed pods are edible but may act as a laxative or emetic if eaten in large quantities. The root bulbs are palatable and nutritious if eaten raw or roasted, but their small size does not justify the death of this delicate, beautiful plant. As a food, glacier lilies are best remembered only for survival purposes.

Medicinal Uses: Although seldom used by modern herbalists, the leaf infusion (tea) of this plant has been shown to be active against a wide spectrum of bacteria, particularly in topical applications. American Indians used various species of glacier lily to reduce fever, swelling, and infection and even to reduce the odds of contraception. In laboratory studies, some of the constituent compounds of *E. grandiflorum* have been shown to have tumor-reducing qualities.

WARNING! Many members of the Lily family share a close resemblance when they are young, and some species are highly toxic. Positive identification may be difficult unless this plant is in full bloom.

Glacier Lily *Erythronium grandiflorum*

Goldenrod
Solidago species

Sunflower Family
Compositae

Goldenrod is a common wayside weed that is easy to identify by its terminal, spire-shaped or triangular clusters of tiny, bright goldenrod yellow flowers. The alternate leaves of the most common species are narrowly lanceolate and may or may not have serrated edges. The plants are erect and range anywhere from 2 inches high (*Solidago multiradiata*, mountain goldenrod) to 70 inches high *(S. canadensis, S. occidentalis, S. gigantea)*. Most species share similar appearances. This is particularly true of the larger species, which may differ only in leaf texture or the presence or absence of stem hairs.

Blooms: June to August.

Habitat and Range: The *Solidago* genus divides into two categories: the species that grow in moist soils and those that prefer drier habitats. Most of the smaller mountain varieties grow in dry soils, often at the edges of forest roads or in open meadows. The larger varieties are common to riparian habitats, irrigated fields, and drainage ditches from below sea level to about 4,000 feet. Several species are widespread across North America, with *S. canadensis* (Canada goldenrod) perhaps the most common.

Edibility: Goldenrod greens may be cooked and eaten like spinach, or they can be added to soups. Their palatability is variable, depending on habitat, age, and personal preferences. The seeds can be used to thicken stews and gravies; the colorful flowers are an attractive salad garnish. The dried-flower tea can be enjoyable, especially when sweetened with honey.

Medicinal Uses: Goldenrod has a well-established history as a medicine, but in current years has been nearly forgotten in North America. The entire plant is widely useful and is still popular as a medicine in Europe. The dried leaves and flowers can be powdered to serve as an excellent styptic agent; in fact, the plant was once known by soldiers of the Crusades as "wound wort" for its ability to stop bleeding on the battlefield. Herbalists past and present know the tea as an effective flu and cold remedy, with actions that help reduce the production of mucus in the bronchi. The tea is also diuretic and is regarded as an excellent kidney tonic. Although labeled a highly allergenic plant, research suggests that goldenrod may be useful in strengthening the body's defenses against allergens at the onset of hay fever season (much like a vaccine).

> **WARNING! Many people are allergic to goldenrod, although in some cases they probably actually are afflicted by the likes of ragweed and other plants sharing the same habitat. Ascertain your sensitivity to this plant before attempting to ingest.**

Canada Goldenrod *Solidago canadensis*

Ground Ivy
Glecoma hederacea

Mint Family
Labiatae

Also known as creeping Charlie for its sprawling growth characteristics, this attractive and potentially useful plant is viewed by many people as a lawn and garden nuisance. Ground ivy is easily identified by its ½- to 1¼-inch, round to kidney-shaped, toothed, opposite leaves and its tubular, pink to blue violet flowers, which are presented in sparse, axillary clusters. The two-lipped flowers have distinctive, dark purple spots and an outward-arching hooded upper lobe that is notched at its tip. The stems are four-sided (square) and characteristically weak, often unable to support the weight of the leaves and causing the plant to "creep" horizontally upon the ground. Unlike many other mints, ground ivy has no discernible odor.

Blooms: March to June, depending mainly on climate.

Habitat and Range: Moist woods and disturbed areas across most of North America. This plant was introduced from Eurasia, and its range continues to spread.

Edibility: Although by some accounts the leaves of this plant are edible (at least in moderation), cases of toxicity in horses have been documented.

Medicinal Uses: Ground ivy is said to possess astringent and expectorant qualities. Traditionally, it was used to combat a variety of respiratory ailments, including various forms of bronchitis, pneumonia, and coughs. Folkloric accounts also claim that a poultice of this plant may be topically useful for bruises, muscle aches, and even cancerous lesions.

> **WARNING! Although no accounts of toxicity in humans have been recorded, ground ivy has proven toxic to horses when consumed in large quantities.**

Harebell
Campanula species

Harebell Family
Campanulaceae

Members of the *Campanula* genus are also collectively known as bluebells, a common name that describes the flowers of this group but is also used universally for several other, completely unrelated blue-flowered plant species. The flowers of this genus have light lavender to dark blue flowers (infrequently white), three stigmas (the pollen-bearing part of the flower), and five petals, which are united to give a bell-like appearance. The leaves are simple and alternate, with *C. rotundifolia* (Scotch harebell) producing petiolate, ovate basal leaves that frequently die back before the plant blooms. Most species of *Campanula* are small plants, seldom taller than 12 inches. They are similar in appearance, particularly their flowers.

Blooms: April to August (depending on altitude and climatic variances).

Habitat and Range: Most members of the *Campanula* clan grow in dry soils at mountain foothill elevations. Several species, including the one illustrated here, are common and widespread across the Northern Hemisphere. Creeping bellflower (*C. rapunculoides*), a large (up to 3 feet tall), taprooted, European import has become a troublesome garden weed in many areas of the United States.

Edibility: The roots are edible, particularly if boiled or sautéed. Although they do not provide enough bulk to justify the death of such a beautiful flower, they have a pleasant nutlike flavor.

Medicinal Uses: A leaf tea of *C. americana* (an eastern North American species) was sometimes used by American Indians as a remedy for tuberculosis and whooping cough. It is seldom employed by contemporary herbalists.

Look-Alike Plants: Harebells have a unique appearance, but an all-too-common name. I have written this profile in favor of the common name "harebell," as opposed to the more frequently used "bluebell" for the purpose of alleviating the common name confusion that exists between *Campanula* species and members of the quite different *Mertensia* genus, and several other blue-flowered plants.

Ground Ivy *Glecoma hederacea*   Harebell *Campanula* species

Hawthorn
Cratageus douglasii

Rose Family
Rosaceae

Hawthorn, a small deciduous tree or large shrub (up to 16 feet tall), is easily recognized and quickly remembered by its nasty 1- to 3-inch curved thorns, which are strategically spaced along the branches—often at eye level. The alternate leaves are narrowly fan-shaped or ovate, presented on short petioles. The margins of the 1- to 2-inch-long leaves are toothed, with the tips of the teeth all pointing distinctly toward the tip of the leaf. The white, ¼-inch flowers form flat, terminate clusters; each blossom has five petals and many stamens. When in full bloom, the flowers may have an unpleasant "dead" odor. In late summer, the flowers are replaced with clusters of red to black berries, each containing two to five seeds.

Blooms: April to June.

Habitat and Range: The *Cratageus* genus is large and varied, with hundreds of species, all of which readily hybridize, in North America. In the West, most species inhabit riparian thickets, where they serve as important forage and nesting habitats for birds and other wildlife. Hawthorns grow from Alaska and British Columbia south into California and throughout the Rocky Mountains.

Edibility: The ripe berries are mildly sweet but tend to lack the juiciness preferred by most berry connoisseurs.

Medicinal Uses: The berries and flowering branches of hawthorn have been used in Chinese medicine for thousands of years. It is regarded as one of the premier heart tonics of herbal medicine, with actions that slightly slow and strengthen the heartbeat while moderating blood pressure. Its usefulness in the treatment of hypertension, arteriosclerosis, angina pectoris, and other heart disorders has been confirmed through centuries of empirical validation and many scientific studies.

Heal-All
Prunella vulgaris

Mint Family
Labiatae

Heal-all is distinguished from other mints by its unique terminal flowers, which are whorled together into a tight, sausage-shaped, purple head. The rest of the plant is characteristic of the Mint family, with the exception that heal-all has no discernible odor. The leaves are opposite, lance shaped, and inconspicuously toothed. The stems are four-sided (square) and structurally weak, a trait that often causes the lower portion of the stem to grow horizontally before growing skyward. This plant varies in size according to climate, soil quality, and available moisture, but expect to see most species within the height range of 3 to 12 inches.

Blooms: May to August.

Habitat and Range: Grows just about anywhere—lawns, roadsides, pastures, and subalpine meadows—but thrives where rich, moist soils have been moderately compacted by livestock, vehicles, or people. Widespread across North America.

Edibility: The entire plant is edible, either raw or cooked. It is best when young and tender. Its flavor is like bland romaine lettuce.

Medicinal Uses: As its common name implies, heal-all (or self-heal) has historically been used as a medicine for just about everything. Modern herbalists regard it as an excellent topical emollient, astringent, and vulnerary agent. It is used in several commercially available all-purpose salves, ointments, and lotions that are intended to soothe and speed the healing of minor burns, wounds, and other irritations. Taken internally, the tea is said to be useful in relieving gastritis and diarrhea, and as an aid in the healing of digestive ulceration. Heal-all contains ursolic acid, a compound that has been shown to have diuretic and antitumor qualities.

Black Hawthorn *Cratageus douglasii*

Heal-All *Prunella vulgaris*

Hedge Nettle
Stachys palustris

Mint Family
Labiatae

Hedge nettle is characterized by its conspicuously fuzzy leaves and stems, and by its white-dotted, reddish purple flowers, which are borne at the upper leaf axils. The lance-shaped or elliptical leaves are 1 to 4 inches long and grow almost directly off the erect stem. The four-sided stems have long hairs growing slightly downward from their angular edges.

Blooms: May to July.

Habitat and Range: Riparian thickets and other consistently moist, shady areas up to about 3,500 feet; widespread across the northern third of the globe, with its range in the western half of North America extending from Alaska south along the coast into southern California and east into Arizona, New Mexico, and the Rocky Mountain States.

Edibility: The leaves and flowers are edible, but their fuzzy texture and bitter taste make this plant unappealing.

Medicinal Uses: Herbalists use hedge nettle as a general-purpose, internal anti-inflammatory medicine. It is used for sore throats, urethritis, cystitis, joint inflammations, and migraine headaches.

Henbit
Lamium amplexicaule

Mint Family
Labiatae

Henbit is typically a small, weedy "lawn and driveway" mint. This annual, a European import, seldom reaches 12 inches when fully mature, and most frequently grows within or slightly above its neighboring ground cover. The opposite leaves are characteristically rounded, with deeply toothed margins. Flowers bloom intermittently from the leaf axils and are pinkish purple, with a lobed and hairy upper lip. *Lamium purpureum* (red henbit or purple dead nettle) and *L. maculatum* (spotted henbit) share similar characteristics but with slight differences, such as the presence of short petioles or the presence of hairs inside the base of the corolla *(L. purpureum)*. Henbit has no discernible odor.

Blooms: Off and on, throughout spring and summer.

Habitat and Range: Cultivated fields, lawns, and other disturbed areas across North America.

Edibility: Although lacking a distinctive flavor, the entire plant is edible. It is an attractive addition to tossed salads, but always beware of the possible presence of herbicides or lawn fertilizers that often accompany henbit's habitat.

Medicinal Uses: Henbit is historically known as a mild but useful astringent and vulnerary herbal medicine. The leaf and flower tea is sometimes used by herbalists to stop minor internal or external bleeding, and to relieve diarrhea and other digestive imbalances. A poultice of the fresh plant is said to help reduce swelling and speed the healing of minor burns, insect stings, and wounds. Scientific research has determined that this plant may be effective as an emmenogogue (an agent that stimulates and assists menstrual bleeding).

Hedge Nettle   *Stachys palustris*

Henbit   *Lamium amplexicaule*

Horehound
Marrubium vulgare

Mint Family
Labiatae

Like most mints, horehound is a perennial with opposite leaves and four-sided stems. But unlike other dryland members of the Labiatae clan, horehound has leaves and stems that are distinctively woolly. The leaves are generally ovate, ½ to 2 inches wide, coarsely textured, and have toothed margins. The flowers are very small, white, and are presented in densely clustered whorls at the leaf axils. The flower bracts are equipped with tiny, sharp spines that effectively adhere to passing people and animals after the plant has dried. Horehound often has no discernible odor, particularly in areas where it grows quickly and profusely with abundant moisture.

Blooms: March to July, depending on climate and other variables.

Habitat and Range: A dryland mint that does especially well in hardpan soils and disturbed areas; introduced from Europe or Asia, now widely but sporadically distributed across North America and throughout much of the world. In the West, it is markedly abundant in the coastal canyons of California and Oregon.

Edibility: Edible but very bitter.

Medicinal Uses: Horehound is perhaps the oldest and most widely recognized herbal cough remedy in today's market, where it is best known as the primary ingredient in many brands of cough drops. The dried leaf and flower tea is used by herbalists for a stronger than usual cough-suppressant or expectorant effect, but the extreme bitterness of this herb quickly educates the user as to why horehound candy is generally preferred.

Horehound *Marrubium vulgare*

Horsetail
Equisetum species

Horsetail Family
Equisetaceae

The Horsetail family is generally divided into three groups: (1) annual varieties with separate and distinctly different fertile and sterile stems; (2) annual varieties with sterile and fertile stems that are similar in appearance; and (3) evergreen perennials with fertile and sterile stems that are alike. Despite variations, the entire family shares fundamentally similar characteristics, including hollow, distinctively grooved and jointed stems, and leaves that are scalelike, dark in color, and appear as sheaths that surround the stems at the joints. The plants reproduce by spores, which are produced in a terminal cone on the fertile plants. For the purpose of introduction we can focus here on two common and widespread species: *Equisetum arvense* (common horsetail) from the first group, and *E. hyemale* (common scouring rush) from the third group. In early spring, *E. arvense* produces a small (3- to 12-inch) fertile stem that lacks chlorophyll. This dies back as its larger, green, sterile counterpart matures. The subsequent sterile stems (6 inches to 2 feet tall) have whorled branches that give the overall appearance of a green bottle brush. *Equisetum hyemale* is much larger (up to 5 feet tall) and lacks any branching characteristics. Its looks like a prehistoric cross between miniature bamboo and an asparagus spear. The two species often grow side-by-side.

Habitat and Range: Lakeshores, streambanks, and other wet areas up into alpine elevations across North America; often the primary groundcover in shady, wet thickets.

Edibility: The roots are edible, as are the young fertile shoots of *E. arvense* when peeled and cooked. The young green shoots of all species are edible when thoroughly boiled but should be consumed only in small quantities (see warning below).

Medicinal Uses: Horsetail contains a considerable amount of calcium and other constituents believed to be collectively useful in the healing of bone fractures and connective tissue injuries. The plant also contains silica, an abrasive compound that makes horsetail an excellent pot scrubber, cleansing hair rinse, or facial scrub. Horsetail tea is used by herbalists as a urinary tract cleanser, and it is often used in the treatment of urinary tract infections. Horsetail is also a traditional herbal remedy for bronchitis and tuberculosis, as it is believed to help strengthen and heal lung tissue. American Indians used horsetail as a diuretic and to help relieve the gum discomforts of teething in children.

> **WARNING! The high silica content in horsetail may irritate the urinary tract and kidneys if used improperly. It is well documented that this plant absorbs heavy metals and chemicals from the soil it lives in. Plants growing at roadside or in the presence of any type of pollution should be avoided. Avoid consumption of the raw plant because horsetail contains thiaminase, an enzyme that destroys vitamin B-1 stored in the body; thorough cooking renders the enzyme harmless.**

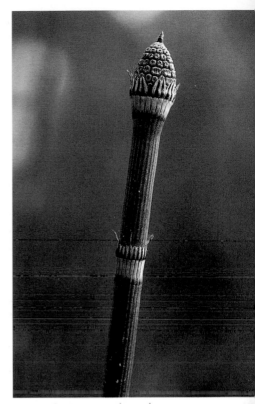

Common Horsetail   *Equisetum arvense*   Horsetail   *Equisetum byemale*

Hound's Tongue
Cynoglossum officinale

Borage Family
Boraginaceae

Hound's tongue is a stout, leafy, taprooted perennial that sometimes grows to a height of 5 feet. The lance-shaped basal leaves have long petioles (leaf stems) and may be 12 inches long. The alternate upper leaves are progressively smaller toward the top of the plant and lack petioles. The flowers are on short, spreading stalks at the top of the plant and are dark purplish red. The fruits are ovate and flat—they look like little hound's tongues—and are covered with tiny prickles that enable them to stick to *anything*. The entire plant is conspicuously hairy.

Blooms: May to July, in the second year of growth.

Habitat and Range: A common roadside weed, particularly common where it is readily transported by livestock; bitterly regarded as a noxious weed across much of North America.

Edibility: Although the young leaves are edible in small amounts after boiling, I strongly discourage the use of this plant as a food.

Medicinal Uses: Most people who desperately try to eradicate it are unaware that hound's tongue is closely related to comfrey (*Symphytum* species), one of the most highly regarded medicinal herbs of all time. For all intents and purposes, these two members of the Borage family are interchangeable. Like comfrey, hound's tongue leaves are sometimes used in salves and poultices to help heal burns, wounds, and irritations of the skin. Its historical, internal uses include it as an anti-inflammatory for the respiratory and digestive systems. It was once widely used in cough remedies when comfrey was not available.

> **WARNING!** Like comfrey, hound's tongue contains a group of potentially carcinogenic alkaloids that may be particularly harmful to the liver if ingested in large quantities. Internal use of this herb is not recommended.

Hound's Tongue   *Cynoglossum officinale*

Hound's Tongue seeds   *Cynoglossum officinale*

Huckleberry

Vaccinium species

Heath Family

Ericaceae

The *Vaccinium* genus is large. More than sixty species and varieties grow in the West (not including the many cultivated varieties of blueberry). The entire lot can be divided into three groups: (1) upland varieties, which prefer well-drained soils and produce dark blue berries *(V. globulare)*; (2) varieties that inhabit bogs and swamps; and (3) varieties with tiny, thin-skinned, often red berries that are deliciously sweet but maddeningly small—too small to collect in any appreciable quantity (*V. scoparium,* grouse whortleberry). All are distinguishable by their alternate, deciduous, broadly lance-shaped leaves; small urn-shaped flowers borne in the leaf axils; and zigzagged stems. The berries, whether red or blue, large or small, have distinctly flattened ends. The most commonly recognized and sought after species are usually dwarf shrubs (up to 3 feet), which bear large (¼- to ½-inch), juicy, sweet blue berries.

Blooms: May to July.

Habitat and Range: Largely a circumboreal plant, huckleberry's range in the western half of North America extends from the Arctic Circle south through the coastal ranges into California and east into the Rocky Mountains of Idaho, Montana, Wyoming, and Colorado. Habitat varies according to species. In mountains of western North America, upland species such as *V. globulare* or the similar *V. membranaceum* are among the most common and widespread. Look for them on cool, densely forested, north-facing hillsides up to alpine elevations, where they will likely be accompanied by a ground-covering mat of the petite grouse whortleberry *(V. scoparium).*

Edibility: The berries of all species are edible, either raw or cooked, and vary in palatability from too tart to sweetly habit-forming. The leaves, when dried, make an excellent, nutritious tea.

Medicinal Uses: Many herbalists maintain that huckleberry-leaf tea may be useful in stabilizing blood sugar levels in cases of diabetes, and medical research has shown that consumption of the leaf extract decreases blood sugar levels shortly after administration. The leaves are believed also to stimulate appetite, and have astringent and antiseptic qualities that are useful in urinary disorders. The leaves and berries are high in vitamin C.

Look-Alike Plants: In the absence of berries, huckleberry is sometimes confused with various other small shrubs. The safest time to introduce yourself to huckleberry is while the plant is producing fruit. Then comes the hard part—diverting your attention from the delicious fruits long enough to take close note of the leaf and stem characteristics. Most plants that are confused with huckleberry have opposite leaves, but huckleberry leaves are always alternate along the stems.

Blue Huckleberry   *Vaccinium globulare*

Indian Paintbrush
Castilleja species

Figwort Family
Scrophulariaceae

Several species of paintbrush inhabit North America, with no fewer than forty-two species in the Pacific Northwest alone. All paintbrushes are characterized by their spikelike terminate flower clusters, which look like a crude brush that has been dipped in paint. Most species produce flowers ranging from yellowish orange to crimson, but a few produce greenish or purple flowers. Regardless of color, the distinctive structure of the inflorescence and the alternating leaves of *Castilleja* are constant throughout the genus.

Blooms: Bloom period varies according to species and ecological niche, but many species are among the first flowers to open in early spring, and often remain in full color throughout the summer.

Habitat and Range: Grasslands and open forest clearings from Alaska to California and throughout New Mexico, Arizona, Nevada, and the Rocky Mountains.

Edibility: Although the flowers may be eaten in small quantities, they tend to absorb selenium, a potentially toxic, alkaline mineral compound. In areas where high amounts of selenium are not present in the soil, Indian paintbrush can be eaten in moderation as a slightly sweet trail snack or salad garnish.

Medicinal Uses: Chippewa Indians used paintbrush to treat rheumatism and as a bath rinse to make their hair glossy (both of these applications were probably related to the selenium content of the plant). Nevada Indians sometimes used dilute solutions of the root tea to treat venereal disease. Various tribes used the flowering plant as its name and appearance suggests—as a paintbrush. Today, it is seldom used as a food or medicine, but some herbalists believe that the selenium content of this plant may make it useful in treating various forms of cancer.

> **WARNING!** Ingestion of paintbrush is not recommended in large quantities, and it should never be consumed from areas where selenium is present in the soil. If you intend to taste this plant, check with your local agricultural authorities about soil content.

Indian Paintbrush   *Castilleja* species

Juniper
Juniperis species

Cypress Family
Cupressaceae

Several species of juniper grow in North America. They comprise a large genus and are differentiated by size (trees or low-growing shrubs) and the specific characteristics of their leaves (needlelike or scalelike). The most widespread variety is common juniper *(Juniperis commonis)*, a ground-hugging shrub with sharp, ¼- to ½-inch needles arranged in whorls of three. Of the tree varieties, western juniper *(J. occidentalis)*, Rocky Mountain juniper *(J. scopulorum)*, and Utah juniper *(J. osteosperma)* are common to their respective habitats in the western United States, often standing out as the predominant foliage in the landscape. Leaves of these varieties are in the "scalelike" category. All junipers can easily be identified by their foliage and cones (the common juniper "berries"), which have a distinctive strong aroma of gin. The conspicuous ¼- to ⅜-inch female berries are a dusty blue and grow from leaf axils (where leaves join branches), where they may remain for two to three years before ripening and falling to the ground. The small, inconspicuous male cones are borne alone at the tips of the branches.

Habitat and Range: Generally a mountain shrub on rocky hillsides and forest clearings up to about 10,000 feet; widespread from Alaska to California and across much of temperate North America. The tree varieties are high-desert dwellers of eastern California, Nevada, Utah, Colorado, Wyoming, Arizona, and New Mexico. Several species of juniper have been domesticated.

Edibility: Juniper berries are the primary ingredient in gin and are frequently used in gourmet recipes; they are especially good for seasoning wild game dishes. In Europe, juniper berries are sometimes used as a pepper substitute.

Medicinal Uses: The leaves and berries have a long-standing empirical reputation among native cultures and herbalists as a strong diuretic and urinary tract disinfectant. Many North American Indian tribes believed that five berries a day, steeped in tea and then ingested, would act as a contraceptive in women. Recent studies suggest that Juniper berries may be useful in treating insulin-dependent diabetes.

Look-Alike Plants: Juniper is sometimes confused with various members of the *Cupressus* (cypress) genus, which has many species with leaves similar to *Juniperis* species. *Cupressus* cones, however, are generally larger and harder, have angular edges, and often have a sharply pointed tip. Once you are familiar with juniper, the ginlike odor of the berries is a dead giveaway.

Utah Juniper (a large shrub or small tree)   *Juniperis osteosperma*

Utah Juniper leaves and berries   *Juniperis osteosperma*
Common Juniper (a needle-leafed shrub variety)   *Juniperis commonis*

Kinnikinnick
Arctostaphylos species

Heath Family
Ericaceae

The *Arctostaphylos* genus may be divided into two categories of evergreen shrubs: small, mat-forming, densely branched groundcovers with woody, trailing stems *(Arctostaphylos uva-ursi)* and small to medium (up to 10 feet tall), erect hardwood shrubs *(A. manzanita)*. Despite size differences, all species present leaf, flower, and fruit characteristics that distinguish them as members of the *Arctostaphylos* clan. The leathery, alternate leaves are spoon to lance shaped, with the upper surfaces darker green than the undersides. The flowers are pink and urn shaped, and are arranged in nodding, few-flowered terminal clusters. The fruits are mealy red berries, which look like tiny (¼- to ½-inch) apples. The name *Arctostaphylos*, from early Greek, translates to "bear berry," another common name for kinnikinnick, which is used universally throughout the genus.

Blooms: April to June. Fruits begin to develop in midsummer.

Habitat and Range: Open forest clearings, from the montane zone up to timberline. *Arctostaphylos uva-ursi* is the predominant circumboreal species, ranging across the northern third of the United States and Canada. In this region, the larger shrub varieties of *Arctostaphylos* are infrequently encountered, but in the mountains of Washington, Oregon, Nevada, Arizona, New Mexico, and particularly California (where manzanita is protected by law), several of the larger shrub varieties (such as *A. manzanita*) predominate.

Edibility: The berries are edible but usually are too tart and mealy to enjoy. Their chief attribute is their hardiness—they often remain in edible condition throughout winter. For this reason, they are best remembered as survival fare.

Medicinal Uses: The common name kinnikinnick is an American Indian word translated as "smoking mixture." The dried leaves of most species were used as a base ingredient in various ceremonial or recreational smoking mixtures. The entire plant is high in tannic acid, and because of this it has a long-standing reputation as an astringent and diuretic medicine. Contemporary herbalists use *A. uva-ursi* as the species of choice for a variety of ailments involving inflammations of the urinary and digestive tracts. Folkloric applications also include kinnikinnick as a remedy for hemorrhoids and postpartum swelling. In these cases, it is used in a sitz bath, a process that involves sitting in 6 inches or more of warm water containing a diluted decoction of *A. uva-ursi*. The effects are simple and predictable—after soaking, the astringent effects are said to reduce pain and swelling of affected tissues.

Kinnikinnick with flowers   *Arctostaphylos uva-ursi*

Bear Berries   *Arctostaphylos uva-ursi*

Knapweed
Centaurea species

Sunflower Family
Compositae

Those of us who do not know knapweed as an invasive and persistent weed may recognize members of the *Centaurea* genus as bachelor's buttons *(C. cyanus)* in the garden. This group of taprooted aliens is generally characterized by purple flowers; strong, fibrous, multibranched stems; and alternate, often pinnately divided leaves.

Blooms: July to October.
Habitat and Range: Highly adaptive; its main requirement is ample sunshine. *Centaurea maculosa* (spotted knapweed), *C. repens* (Russian knapweed), and *C. pratensis* (meadow knapweed) are intensely invasive and potentially damaging to native habitats. In many areas of the West, knapweed is profusely abundant in rangelands and has earned a permanent place on the Top Ten Noxious Weeds List. It may have been introduced from grain crops imported from Russia during the early part of this century.
Edibility: Not edible.
Medicinal Uses: Knapweed has been used as a topical vulnerary, sore throat remedy, and appetite stimulant from as far back as the fourteenth century. Herbalists recognize *C. cyanus* as a powerful nervine that may relieve discomforts relative to nerve impairment, and American Indians used it for venomous bites, indigestion, jaundice, and eye disorders. The seventeenth-century herbalist Nicholas Culpeper wrote, "It [knapweed] gently heals up running sores, both cancerous and fistulous, and will do the same for scabs of the head." Although the techniques and theories set forth by phyto-medical pioneers such as Culpeper are "therapeutically questionable" in the minds of contemporary medical researchers, the long and empirically validated history of knapweed as a versatile weapon against disease should at least warrant further investigation through the eyes of modern science. After all, knapweed is here to stay, and what healthier alternative could we have than to use it for our well-being?

Lamb's Quarter
Chenopodium album

Goosefoot Family
Chenopodiaceae

This common annual weed is characterized first by its leaves and second by its unique flowers. The upper surfaces of the alternate, triangular- to spade-shaped leaves are darker than their undersides, have toothed or lobed margins, and surfaces covered with tiny silver scales, giving the entire plant a lightly powdered-sugar appearance. The drab, inconspicuous flowers look like little green, mealy lint balls, and are clustered in the leaf axils at the top of the plant. Mature plants may reach 5 feet tall.

Blooms: March to July.
Habitat and Range: Gardens, cultivated fields, and other disturbed sites across North America.
Edibility: Lamb's quarter is often among the myriad of springtime weeds we discard from the garden, but it is also one of the best tasting and most nutritious wild greens. Although best when young and tender, the leaves are enjoyable through most of the growth season. The flavor is much like spinach, and the plucked leaves are excellent in salads, sauces (pesto!), or as a cooked green. *Chenopodium ambrosioides*, a common Southwest species, is known by Mexican food epicureans as *epazote* and is used as a primary spice in several Southwest dishes. *Epazote* resembles lamb's quarter, but has glossy leaves. The seeds of all species should not be ingested.

Medicinal Uses: American Indians used the leaves to prevent scurvy and to treat stomachaches. A poultice of the leaves was used to treat burns. The seeds of *C. ambrosioides* were sometimes used to expel roundworms, a practice that should be attempted only with the advice of a qualified practitioner.

WARNING! Although the leaves of lamb's quarter are safe and nutritious in any quantity, the seeds may lead to toxic effects if consumed.

Spotted Knapweed   *Centaurea maculosa*   Lamb's Quarter   *Chenopodium album*

Licorice

Glycyrrhiza lepidota

Pea Family
Leguminosae

Wild licorice is a large (up to 3 feet) perennial member of the Pea family easily differentiated from other wild legumes by its unique seed pods and its erect, branching stature. The ½- to ¾-inch seed pods are covered by a profusion of hooked spines and are presented in dense, sticky clusters. No other wild, North American legume shares this characteristic. Almost as a courtesy to the wild plant enthusiast, the seed pods often are present through the winter months, which makes early spring identification easy. The alternate leaves are pinnately divided seven to nineteen times into lance-shaped leaflets, which often develop glandular dots on their surfaces. The flowers are greenish white and are presented in elongated clusters on long peduncles (flower stems) arising from the leaf axils.

Blooms: June to August.

Habitat and Range: Disturbed sites, particularly in roadside ditches and at the edges of cultivated fields, across most of North America.

Edibility: American Indians used the roots as a cooking spice and often chewed them (raw) as a trail snack. If you choose to eat the roots, do not expect a strong licorice flavor. Although North American *Glycyrrhiza lepidota* is useful, the Eurasian species, *G. glabra,* and the Chinese *G. uralensis* are much stronger and represent the primary market varieties. Both imported varieties have escaped cultivation in isolated areas of the West.

Medicinal Uses: In Chinese medicine, licorice root has ranked as one of the most important and versatile medicines for several thousand years. Many scientific studies have validated its usefulness. It is known to have anti-inflammatory effects that mimic cortisone in the body, without the dangerous side effects associated with most steroid drugs. The active ingredient in this remarkable plant is glycyrrhizin, a compound believed to be effective as an antiallergenic, anticonvulsive, antibacterial, and antispasmodic medicine. Licorice root has been successfully used in the treatment of asthma, stomach ulcers, bronchitis, and urinary tract disorders. It is believed to be useful in weakening the effects of toxic substances in the body. In Chinese studies of cough suppression medicines, licorice root was as effective as codeine, the popular antitussive narcotic found in several prescription and over-the-counter cough remedies.

WARNING! Prolonged use of large doses of licorice may cause water retention and elevated blood pressure.

Wild Licorice   *Glycyrrhiza lepidota*
Inset: The unique seed pods of *G. lepidota* make it easy to identify.

Louisewort

Pedicularis species

Figwort Family
Scrophulariaceae

Also known as elephant's-head or betony, this attractive and unique genus of perennials is characterized by its flowers, leaves, and unusual growth characteristics. The flowers of this genus (particularly *Pedicularis groenlandica*) look like tiny elephant heads, range in color from white to yellow to pink, and are borne in a terminal, spikelike inflorescence. The alternate leaves are toothed or pinnately divided, commonly resembling fern fronds. Adding to this plant's unique qualities is its tendency to be parasitic. Its roots often attach to the roots of a host plant, drawing nutrients from them.

Blooms: May to August, dependent mainly on altitude and climatic conditions.

Habitat and Range: Habitat varies between species, but most grow in moist meadows of the montane and subalpine zones. *Pedicularis groenlandica* thrives across the northern third of North America and south in the West to the mountains of California and New Mexico. *Pedicularis contorta,* a dryland variety, ranges throughout the Rocky Mountains and Sierra foothills. More than two dozen other species inhabit the western United States.

Edibility: Provided that lousewort is not attached to an unpalatable host, the fleshy roots can be prepared and eaten in moderation. The flavor is similar to parsnips. The sweet flowers were sometimes enjoyed by Inuit Indian children as a special "candy" treat. The leaves and stems may be steamed or boiled as a potherb, but precautionary measures are necessary before ingesting this plant.

Medicinal Uses: Lousewort's use as a medicine dates back to at least the seventeenth century, when it was used in Europe for stomach ulcers, rheumatism, and urinary problems. Ojibwa Indians even used it as an aphrodisiac, an action that is likely attributable to a mild irritation of the urinary tract. Contemporary herbalists recognize betony as a mild sedative and muscle relaxant, useful in treating cases of physical overexertion.

> **WARNING!** Due to the parasitic tendencies of lousewort, you must be particularly aware of the identity and nature of the host. *Pedicularis* will pick up the characteristics of whatever it is attached to, including toxic substances. Because of the sedative nature of this plant and the trace presence of potentially toxic alkaloids, moderation and experience must accompany its medicinal use.

Lousewort *Pedicularis groenlandica*   Lousewort *Pedicularis contorta*

Maidenhair Fern
Adiantum pedatum

Common Fern Family
Polypodiaceae

Maidenhair fern is easily distinguished from other ferns by its wiry, shiny black or dark brown stems, which stand out in bold contrast to the plant's delicate green leaves. The fifteen to forty individual leaflets (pinnules) of each pinnately compounded leaf (frond) are uniquely lobed on one side to give each the appearance of a miniature fan.

Habitat and Range: Three species of maidenhair fern inhabit the West; all are partial to cool, moist, undisturbed forests, especially where old-growth cedars are present. The most common species, *Adiantum pedatum*, ranges throughout temperate woodlands of North America. *Adiantum jordanii* (California maidenhair) ranges primarily throughout the coastal mountains of California. *Adiantum capillus-veneris* (Venus-haired fern), is infrequently encountered in warmer mountain areas of the West.

Edibility: The young shoots (also known as fiddleheads) are edible when young and tightly coiled. Once they begin to uncoil and stand up, they become somewhat toxic. The fiddleheads produced by this plant are very small, however, and their food value and palatability generally do not justify the damage caused by harvesting them.

Medicinal Uses: Native Americans sometimes chewed the leaves of this plant to stop internal bleeding. In Europe, it has a long history as a menstrual stimulant, and contemporary herbalists claim its usefulness as a mild cough suppressant, particularly in cases where airborne irritants are the primary cause of distress. The leaf tea was often used by American Indians as a hair rinse, to add shine and body.

Mallow
Malva neglecta

Mallow Family
Malvaceae

Common mallow is another of those "profusely common vacant lot weeds" whose usefulness is essentially overlooked because of its invasiveness. The leaves of this annual or biennial plant are characteristic of the family: nearly round or heart shaped, 1 to 4 inches wide, with five to seven lobes. The flowers are five-petaled, cup shaped, pale lavender to white, and are borne from the leaf axils in sparse clusters. The fruits are the most distinctive feature of the plant, but are usually shrouded from view by the leaves. Each one is a round, flattened capsule similar in appearance to a tiny (½ inch) wheel of green cheese.

Blooms: Often perpetual throughout the spring and summer growth season of the plant.

Habitat and Range: A European import that makes its home in gardens and disturbed areas across North America.

Edibility: The entire plant is edible; the young leaves are best when added to salads or prepared as a potherb. Mallow has a slippery-sticky, mucilaginous quality (similar to okra) that makes it useful as a thickening agent in soups and gravies. The fruits have a flavor somewhat like cheese, which (coupled with their appearance) has earned the plant the common name "cheese weed."

Medicinal Uses: Mallow root is highly regarded by herbalists as an effective demulcent and emollient. Both of these actions are attributed to the plant's mucilaginous qualities. It is used topically to soothe skin irritations and internally to remedy respiratory and digestive ailments. Although closely related, *Malva neglecta* is not the same plant as the much larger marsh mallow *(Althea officinalis)*, a plant cultivated commercially to serve identical medicinal purposes.

Maidenhair Fern   *Adiantum pedatum*

Common Mallow   *Malva neglecta*

Meadowsweet
Spiraea species

Rose Family
Rosaceae

The *Spiraea* genus consists of small (up to 6 feet) deciduous shrubs characterized by diminutive but showy, white to red, five-petaled flowers presented in densely clustered, flat-topped or spikelike terminal inflorescences. The stigmas of the tiny blossoms often protrude above the petals, giving the flower clusters an overall fuzzy appearance. The alternate leaves are toothed from about midleaf forward to the tip, with the undersides lighter than the upper surfaces. The stems are strong and woody and often look jointed or angular along their lengths. The fruits are presented as inconspicuous clusters of tiny, dry capsules.

Blooms: June to August.

Habitat and Range: Several species of meadowsweet inhabit mountainous areas throughout western North America, from Alaska south. Habitat varies somewhat among species, but much of this genus may be found at the margins of forest clearings and in moist draws up to alpine elevations. A few varieties have been cultivated for use as ornamental landscape shrubs.

Edibility: Not edible.

Medicinal Uses: Meadowsweet is a reliable source of methyl salicylate, a compound similar to the primary active ingredient in aspirin. Unlike other salicylate-bearing plants, such as willow or poplar, meadowsweet's content of this analgesic compound remains consistent from plant to plant. Aside from the plant's value in relieving pain, inflammation, and fever, meadowsweet also has a reputation for relieving a variety of stomach disorders—an attribute not offered by aspirin. Blackfeet Indians used the tea as an enema, vaginal douche, and to treat various forms of venereal disease.

Milkweed
Asclepias species

Milkweed Family
Asclepiadaceae

Milkweeds are characterized by their umbrella-shaped, pink to reddish purple flower clusters and fleshy leaves and roots, which contain a sticky, milky sap. The leaves of this mainly perennial group of plants have short petioles and are presented in opposite pairs or closely arranged spokelike whorls *(Asclepias fascicularis)*. The leaves range in shape between narrowly and broadly lanceolate, according to species. Leaf shape is an important characteristic to bear in mind if you wish to employ milkweed as a food or medicine, as the narrow-leafed varieties (such as *A. fascicularis*) tend to be overly toxic. Showy milkweed *(A. speciosa)* is our largest milkweed and is perhaps the easiest of the broad-leaved varieties to recognize, often standing in bold contrast to surrounding plants with its large leaves (up to 8 inches long) and showy, five-petaled, purplish red flowers.

Blooms: May to July.

Habitat and Range: Well described as "ditch plants," typically growing at the edges of roadways or in moist soils at the edges of cultivated fields or riparian habitats. *Asclepias speciosa* ranges from British Columbia to California, generally below 4,000 feet. *Asclepias syriaca* (common milkweed), a widely distributed broad-leaved species of eastern North America, closely resembles showy milkweed.

Edibility: Although the leaves of this plant are edible, milkweed should be approached as a food only after it is thoroughly cooked, and then with caution and moderation. The milky sap contains compounds that may cause severe nausea if ingested raw or in large quantities. The toxicity of this plant is removed after boiling the leaves in two or more changes of water, but the flavor is nothing to rave about. The flowers have a high sugar content and were sometimes cooked down into a syrup by American Indians.

Medicinal Uses: Milkweed enjoys a long and diverse history as a medicine. The milky sap was traditionally used to eliminate warts and skin parasites, and the roots were decocted for use in treating maladies ranging from constipation to venereal disease, kidney stones, asthma, and even cancer. In the 1880s, the plant was adopted by the Canadian pharmaceutical industry as an antiseptic. Native Americans used the plant as a contraceptive and snakebite remedy. Today, herbalists use the roots of milkweed primarily as a respiratory expectorant.

> **WARNING!** Milkweed is potentially toxic if consumed in large enough quantities. Narrow-leafed species tend to be more toxic than the broad-leafed species.

Meadowsweet *Spiraea betulifolia*

Showy Milkweed *Asclepias speciosa*

Monkeyflower

Figwort Family

Mimulus species

Scrophulariaceae

This large and varied genus of annual and perennial herbs is best remembered by its habitat and flower characteristics. Most perennial varieties grow in permanently moist soils, often sharing habitat with such plants as watercress, coltsfoot, speedwell, and cattail. The habitats of the annual varieties are more varied and generally drier, but nonetheless moist—damp, open meadows, for example. The blossoms of monkeyflowers are often likened to the shape of a laughing monkey face, but I find that some imagination is required to establish this as a reliable field reference. Imagination aside, the yellow, red, or purple flowers flare at the mouth to form two upper lips and three lower lips; they have four stamens and are borne from the axils of the upper leaves. The alternate leaves range in shape from lance shaped to nearly round, and in most instances have short (almost absent) petioles. Most monkeyflowers are small plants, seldom more than 12 inches high. One exception is *Mimulus guttatus*, which may grow to 30 inches.

Blooms: May to August (variable according to climate and elevation).

Habitat and Range: Permanently wet or moist areas up to timberline. Several species of monkeyflower range throughout the West from Alaska to Mexico.

Edibility: The leaves and stems of this plant taste salty and were used by Native Americans as a flavor enhancer. Although the raw leaves tend to be bitter, cooking improves their flavor.

Medicinal Uses: The cool juice of monkeyflower's foliage makes it useful as a soothing poultice for minor burns and skin irritations.

Miner's Lettuce

Purslane Family

Montia species

Portulacaceae

Miner's lettuce is easily distinguished by its peculiar upper stem leaves, which completely surround the stems in joined pairs, a characteristic that makes them look like tiny lily pads. The flowers are tiny, either axillary or terminate, and range from white to pale pink. The entire plant is seldom more than 1 foot high. Other *Montia* species, such as the perennial candyflower *(M. [Claytonia] cordifolia)*, share more subtle characteristics; they all have five-petaled flowers and succulent, glabrous (hairless) leaves and stems.

Blooms: Early to midspring.

Habitat and Range: All *Montia* species prefer moist soils. *Montia perfoliata* is common to gardens, lawns, pastures, and other disturbed areas. *Montia (Claytonia) cordifolia* and other perennial species inhabit forests, preferring shade and requiring ample moisture. *Montia perfoliata* is widespread from British Columbia south to Baja, and east from the Pacific to the eastern edges of the Rockies. *Montia cordifolia* can be found throughout most of British Columbia and the United States Northwest, and into northern Utah. Several other species are distributed throughout much of the Mountain and Pacific West.

Edibility: Of all edible plants, miner's lettuce stands out as one of the most palatable. Named for its use by miners of the California gold rush, the leaves and stems of this group of plants taste almost identical to lettuce and are excellent in sandwiches and salads. Unlike most other wild edibles, which become tough and bitter with age, miner's lettuce stays tender and sweet throughout its growth cycle.

Medicinal Uses: The crushed leaves and stems (a poultice) of any *Montia* species are cooling and soothing when applied to minor burns and skin irritations. Songish Indians used the plant in this fashion to relieve headache.

Yellow Monkeyflower   *Mimulus guttatus*   Candyflower   *Montia (Claytonia) cordifolia*

Miner's Lettuce   *Montia perfoliata*

Motherwort

Leonurus cardiaca

Mint Family
Labiatae

Like most mints, motherwort has opposite leaves, four-sided (square) stems, and flowers borne in densely whorled clusters at the upper leaf axils. Unlike any other mint, motherwort has deeply lobed, coarsely toothed palmate leaves that are uniquely its own, making it easy to distinguish from other mints. All of the leaves are borne from the stems (there are no branches) and are progressively smaller toward the top of the plant, which may grow to 60 inches tall. Motherwort has no discernible minty odor.

Blooms: April to July.

Habitat and Range: Habitat varies, the only requirement being rich, moist soil. Once this plant has become established, it often grows in profusion but seldom ventures far from its point of introduction. A twenty-acre plot of land may be virtually covered by this plant, without another specimen for hundreds of miles. An import from Asia, motherwort has sporadically established itself across much of North America.

Edibility: Not recognized as edible.

Medicinal Uses: *Leonurus cardiaca* means "lion's heart" and derives from the plant's ancient history as a Chinese and Western herbal medicine. It is used to tone the heart muscle and has been shown to slow and strengthen the heartbeat while lowering high blood pressure. The common name motherwort is also derived from the plant's medicinal attributes, as it has been used for centuries as a uterine antispasmodic and tonic. Motherwort is said to possess diuretic, sedative, and analgesic qualities. The effectiveness and safety of this plant have been well documented in Chinese clinical and laboratory studies.

Motherwort   *Leonurus cardiaca*

The unique leaf of motherwort makes it easy to distinguish from other mints.

Mullein
Verbascum thapsus

Figwort Family
Scrophulariaceae

This conspicuous biennial is recognized during its first year of growth as a basal rosette of large (up to 12 inches long), broadly lance-shaped, profusely fuzzy leaves. During its second and final year of growth, mullein heads skyward with a stout, central stalk that may exceed 6 feet. The many yellow flowers form a terminate, coblike inflorescence. As the flowers dry, each forms a capsule containing multitudes of tiny seeds (each about the size of a table salt granule). Once the capsules begin to open, the seeds are generously released by wind, precipitation, or the slightest disturbance of a passerby.

Blooms: Throughout summer.

Habitat and Range: A Eurasian import that has made itself at home in any variety of disturbed sites across North America, where it often serves as an important "earth regenerator," helping to reestablish biological balances and to prevent erosion.

Edibility: The leaves are edible in small quantities when cooked, but their woolly texture makes them undesirable to most palates.

Medicinal Uses: American Indians dried the leaves and smoked them to relieve the symptoms of asthma and other respiratory discomforts. The leaf tea is recognized by herbalists around the world as a traditional remedy for respiratory congestion and hemorrhage. The flowers are said to possess strong antimicrobial qualities, and are especially well known for their use (as an oil infusion) in the treatment of ear infections. The root is believed to have astringent and tonic qualities that make it useful in treating urinary incontinence. The seeds were used by American Indians as a paralytic fish poison, as they contain a considerable amount of rotenone.

> **WARNING!** Although no adverse side effects have been noted with mullein, it contains coumarin and rotenone, two substances that may prove toxic if ingested in large enough quantities. The seeds should not be consumed under any circumstances.

Nettle-Leafed Horsemint
Agastache urticifolia

Mint Family
Labiatae

This large (up to 5 feet) perennial is also referred to as giant hyssop, as the plant shares a striking resemblance to its garden-variety relative, *Hyssopus officinalis*. Like all mints, nettle-leafed horsemint has opposite leaves. The stems are characteristically four-sided (square) as well. Unlike many other mints, which have axillary flowers, nettle-leafed horsemint bears its small, purplish white flowers in terminate, 1- to 4-inch-long, sausage-shaped spires. The 1- to 3-inch leaves of nettle-leafed horsemint are broadly lance shaped or triangular, with toothed margins, much like the leaves of stinging nettle (*Urtica* species). The entire plant has a strong, almost skunklike pungency. The similar *Agastache foeniculum* (lavender hyssop) has more oblong leaves and an aniselike odor.

Blooms: June to August.

Habitat and Range: Inhabits dry, sunny areas at foothill elevations from British Columbia south to California, and east into the Rocky Mountains. *Agastache foeniculum* extends from much of the same region into central Canada.

Edibility: The dried leaves make an enjoyable tea, provided it is brewed weakly.

Medicinal Uses: The Lakota Indian name for this plant is *wahpé yatápi*, meaning "leaf that is chewed." Cheyenne Indians used the leaf tea for chest pains and to strengthen a weak heart. Indians and modern herbalists recognize the leaf and flower tea as a carminative (to expel intestinal gas), diaphoretic (to induce sweating), and mild sedative.

Mullein (second year)   *Verbascum thapsus*

Mullein flowers   *Verbascum thapsus*

Nettle-Leafed Horsemint   *Agastache urticifolia*

Oregon Grape

Berberis (Mahonia) species

Barberry Family

Berberidaceae

The first point of reference to remember in the identification of this evergreen perennial is its close resemblance to holly *(Ilex opaca)*, the Christmas green. Much like holly, the durable, almost plastic-textured pinnate leaves of Oregon grape tend to turn red after a heavy frost, have sharp spines at their margins, and show glossy upper surfaces that are darker than the undersides. The second point of reference in the identification of this plant is the juicy, red to purple, ¼-inch berries, which grow in narrowly arranged clusters like tiny grapes. The berries are preceded by bright yellow flowers presented in five whorls that each contain three small flowers. The strong, woody stems form low-growing foliage in most species, with the exception of *Berberis aquifolium*, which grows as a small, erect shrub. Most species (such as *B. repens*) are rhizomatous ground covers, and are often found in spreading colonies of root-borne offshoots where soils and forest matter are resilient enough to allow its subterranean sprawl. *Berberis nervosa* is a horizontal crawler as well, but presents itself above ground in a rosette fashion.

Blooms: May to July.

Habitat and Range: *Berberis nervosa* and *B. repens* grow in coniferous forests up to timberline from the Pacific Coast to the eastern slopes of the Rockies, north from British Columbia and Alberta and south into the mountains of central California, Colorado, New Mexico, and points in between. *Berberis aquifolium* primarily inhabits the coastal forests and foothills of the Northwest, except where it has been introduced as a landscape shrub.

Edibility: Although sour, the ripe berries are edible either raw or cooked. They are high in vitamin C, and when prepared with an ample quantity of sugar, make a good jelly. They are an important source of forage for a wide variety of birds and mammals.

Medicinal Uses: The roots, stems, and leaves of this plant contain a substantial amount of the bright yellow, bitter alkaloid berberine. Berberine is known to possess strong antimicrobial qualities, and for this reason early peoples and modern herbalists alike have recognized this plant as an aid in fighting infection, both topically and internally. Berberine is also well known for stimulating bile production, and for this purpose it has been used for centuries to treat a variety of liver and digestive disorders. Several Indian tribes used the roots to produce a bright, goldenrod yellow dye. Herbalists regard Oregon grape as an excellent alternative to goldenseal, a plant that is seriously threatened due to overharvesting.

Oregon Grape berries *Berberis repens*

Oregon Grape *Berberis aquifolium*

The alkaloid berberine gives the inner root bark its rich, goldenrod yellow color.

Oxeye Daisy
Chrysanthemum leucanthemum

Sunflower Family
Compositae

Common to roadsides and waste areas, oxeye daisy at first glance looks like any other white daisy. But close examination of this plant's unique leaf characteristics makes it easy to differentiate from all other daisies, during any stage of its perennial growth cycle. The basal leaves have proportionately long petioles (leaf stems) and are spoon shaped, with rounded teeth at their margins. This characteristic makes oxeye daisy easy to recognize anytime, even when the plant first emerges as an otherwise inconspicuous low-growing rosette of leaves. The leaves on the upper plant lack petioles, and the flowers are typically daisylike—white with yellow centers and up to 3 inches wide. The entire plant may reach a height of 3 feet.

Blooms: First in early summer, then typically remaining in bloom until fall.

Habitat and Range: A Eurasian import that is now common to roadsides and dry waste areas across the northern half of North America, up to about 6,000 feet.

Edibility: Oxeye daisy is generally overlooked as "just another wayside weed," but the leaves of this plant are among the most palatable fresh wild greens available. The young basal leaves are best and have a sweet flavor with a texture much like romaine lettuce; gourmet restaurants sometimes serve them in salads.

Medicinal Uses: Again, this useful plant is universally and unjustly overlooked. The leaves are recognized by some contemporary herbalists for their diuretic and hemostatic qualities. Clinical research suggests that the leaf tea may also be useful as an antihistamine medicine that slows the body's responses to allergens while helping to reduce excess secretions of mucus. The flowers contain pyrethrins, compounds useful (and commercially produced) in making safe, natural insecticides.

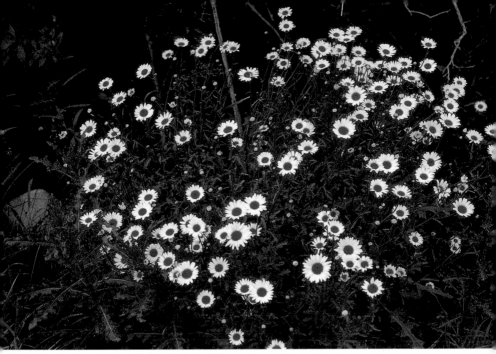

Oxeye Daisy   *Chrysanthemum leucanthemum*

The distinctive basal leaves of oxeye daisy.

Pearly Everlasting
Anaphalis margaritacea

Sunflower Family
Compositae

Pearly everlasting is distinguished by its terminate, spikelike or nearly umbrella-shaped clusters of small (¼- to ½-inch) globe-shaped flowers, each with tiny, papery white petals and a yellow center. The alternate leaves are narrowly lance shaped, with undersides covered with white, woolly hairs. The stems of the plant, too, are woolly, giving the plant an overall gray green appearance. The basal leaves usually die back as the plant matures. Roots are in the form of extensive, perennial rhizomes. The size of this plant varies greatly between habitats, but you can expect to find pearly everlasting within the range of 6 to 12 inches.

Blooms: May to August.

Habitat and Range: Generally a mountain plant; ranges throughout most of western North America in just about any variety of montane habitat up to timberline; seems to prefer road margins, clearcuts, burn sites, and other disturbed areas.

Edibility: Not recognized as edible.

Medicinal Uses: American Indians of the Pacific Northwest used this plant to treat tuberculosis and to expel intestinal worms. Chippewa Indians smudged it with mint and used it as a treatment for paralysis. The entire plant was sometimes made into an infusion and applied as a healing wash for external wounds, and Mohawk Indians used the infused flowers as treatment for asthma. Today, it is recognized by herbalists for its mild antihistamine actions and is sometimes applied as an astringent and anti-inflammatory remedy for swollen mucous membranes. It is also said to possess expectorant, diaphoretic, and mild sedative qualities.

Look-Alike Plants: Pearly everlasting is often confused with members of the *Gnaphalium* (cudweed) genus and the *Antennaria* (pussytoes) genus. The characteristic that differentiates pearly everlasting from the cudweeds is its rhizomatous (horizontally growing) root system—cudweeds have taproots that go straight down. The differences between *Anaphalis* and members of the pussytoes clan are more subtle, but still easy to recognize. Pearly everlasting is generally a larger plant with larger stem leaves, and the die-back characteristic of pearly everlasting's basal leaves is always a dead giveaway.

Periwinkle
Vinca major, V. minor

Dogbane Family
Apocynaceae

Periwinkle is an attractive perennial vine with glossy, dark green, oval or broadly lance-shaped opposite leaves. The showy blue or lavender flowers have five petals and range in diameter from ¾ to 1½ inches.

Blooms: March to August, depending on conditions. In areas with consistently mild climates (such as southern California), periwinkle may remain in bloom throughout the spring and summer months.

Habitat and Range: A cultivated, ground-covering shade plant that was introduced from Europe and has found its way out of flower beds across North America; particularly abundant in coastal areas of the western United States, where in many cases it has taken over the real estate it was originally intended to adorn.

Edibility: Not recognized as edible.

Medicinal Uses: Periwinkle is regarded among herbalists as a strong capillary constrictor, useful for treating various types of hemorrhage. It is also believed to have hypotensive qualities and is sometimes used for treating migraine headaches. Recent scientific studies suggest that certain periwinkle species may inhibit cancerous tumor growth.

Pearly Everlasting   *Anaphalis margaritacea*

Common Periwinkle   *Vinca major*

Pineapple Weed
Matricaria matricarioides

Sunflower Family
Compositae

This delightful annual is widely known as "wild chamomile," as it shares a similar appearance and aroma with its close but domesticated relative, chamomile. The primary difference between the appearance of pineapple weed and chamomile is the flower. Chamomile has yellow-centered flowers with white rays (like a tiny daisy), but in pineapple weed flowers, all rays are absent. The sweet, pineapple-like aroma of pineapple weed arises immediately at the slightest disturbance of the plant, and once experienced, it is quickly and delightfully remembered.

Blooms: Throughout spring and early summer; a very successful reproducer, dropping multitudes of minuscule seeds throughout its bloom cycle.

Habitat and Range: Pineapple weed's habitual tendencies lean toward the masochistic, as it seems to prefer the center of footpaths, highway shoulders, and other high-impact areas with poor, tightly compacted soils. It ranges throughout the West, from central Alaska to California and east throughout the Rocky Mountains.

Edibility: The dried flowers of this plant make a delicious tea almost identical in flavor to chamomile. The leaves are edible as well, but tend to be bitter.

Medicinal Uses: Again, identical to chamomile. The tea is carminative, antispasmodic to the stomach, and mildly sedative, helping to expel gas from the digestive tract and to prevent heartburn while acting to subtly soothe the nerves. In other words, it might help after drinking the scalding cup of burnt coffee that washed down the ninety-nine-cent green chili burrito you consumed in two bites while driving to a tax audit in rush hour traffic.

Look-Alike Plants: Mayweed chamomile *(Anthemis cotula)* closely resembles pineapple weed, but has an unpleasant odor and white ray flowers.

Pipsissewa
Chimaphila umbellata

Heath Family
Ericaceae

Also known as prince's pine, this small (up to 12 inches tall) evergreen perennial is distinguished by its leathery, lance-shaped leaves, which grow directly off the woody stems in spokelike whorls. The waxy, almost plastic-looking, pink, ½- to ¾-inch flowers each have five petals and five sepals and are borne on terminal stalks that extend above the rest of the plant. Pipsissewa reproduces primarily from its extensive rhizomes, which often form dense colonies of offshoot plants in areas where deep, undisturbed forest compost allows the roots to creep about freely.

Blooms: May to July.

Habitat and Range: Prefers shaded, coniferous forests where compost is deep and environmental impact is minimal. In deforested areas or other areas of heavy human use, pipsissewa grows beneath decomposing logs or directly beside a tree. Ranges from Alaska south to the high mountains of southern California, and east across the northern third of North America.

Edibility: Although the leaves are edible, their astringency and tough structure makes them unappealing.

Medicinal Uses: American Indians used this plant for kidney stones, bladder inflammations, and as an astringent eyewash for sore eyes. Modern scientific studies have confirmed the usefulness of this plant as a diuretic and urinary astringent-disinfectant. It is popular among holistic practitioners as a safe, dependable remedy for cystitis and other bladder disorders. Much to its misfortune, pipsissewa is also a "secret ingredient" in certain popular soft drinks; in many areas of the United States Northwest, the plants are disappearing under commercial pressures at an alarming rate (see pyrola).

Pineapple Weed   *Matricaria matricarioides*

Pipsissewa, or Prince's Pine   *Chimaphila umbellata*

Plantain

Plantago major

Plantain Family
Plantaginaceae

Common plantain is an annual or perennial herb characterized by its low-growing rosette of broad leaves and its rather drab but distinctive flower cluster. The succulent but sturdy leaves are on proportionately long petioles (leaf stems) and have distinct parallel veins that contain strong fibers. The flowers are small and inconspicuous, borne in tightly arranged sausage-shaped spikes atop leafless stalks that reach well above the rest of the plant. Ten or more species of the *Plantago* genus inhabit western North America, with common plantain *(P. major)* by far the most widespread and abundant. Leaf configurations vary between species, from egg shaped *(P. major)* to narrowly linear *(P. patagonica, P. psyllium, P. elongata)*. Most plantain species share a fairly similar appearance, most notably in their terminate flowers atop leafless stalks.

Blooms: March to August.

Habitat and Range: Prefers high-impact areas and frequently grows down the center of dirt roads, in walkways, and even in cracks in highways; widespread across most of North America.

Edibility: Plantain is one of many useful plants that have been forgotten because of its abundance and its reputation as a weed. Many of us will step on it en route to the vegetable garden, unaware that it may be more nutritious than the vegetables we tend. In fact, plantain was probably introduced from Eurasia as a food crop, and although tough and fibrous, the entire plant is edible (raw or cooked), with a flavor similar to Swiss chard. The strong leaf fibers can easily be removed after boiling the herbage, a practice that greatly improves the leaves' palatability. Plantain is high in vitamins C, A, and K.

Medicinal Uses: *Plantago psyllium* is widely known for its seeds, which are used as an effective laxative and a source of dietary fiber. The leaves contain mucilaginous constituents that are well known by modern herbalists and folkloric practitioners for their soothing, anti-inflammatory qualities. The crushed leaves are applied topically in poultices to soothe and heal minor irritations and wounds. Internally, the plant is used to relieve discomforts of the digestive tract. In survival situations, the remarkably strong leaf fibers of the mature plant can be peeled away from the leaf veins for use as thread, fishing line, or even suture material. The seeds of all species have been shown to reduce blood cholesterol levels.

Look-Alike Plants: When young, plantains resemble many members of the Lily family, a group of plants that includes several toxic members. The distinct leaf veins, and especially the flowers of plantain, make for positive identification. When in doubt, wait until this plant blooms.

Common Plantain *Plantago major*

Poplar
Populus species

Willow Family
Salicaceae

Poplars are deciduous trees or large shrubs characterized by their catkin-type unisexual flowers, their sharply pointed, broadly lanceolate to nearly ovate, long-petioled leaves, and the consistently moist habitats where they live. The drooping male and female catkins are borne on separate plants. Black cottonwood *(Populus trichocarpa)* and quaking aspen *(P. tremuloides)* are among the most widely distributed and readily recognized species in North America, and they serve as excellent examples from which to base your familiarity with the rest of the *Populus* clan. Black cottonwood is a large tree (up to 120 feet) that often stands predominantly in its riparian habitat. The leaves are broadly oval with distinctively pointed tips and have undersides that appear almost white, with rust-colored veins. The bark of the young tree is white and smooth, later becoming gray-brown, thick, and deeply furrowed as the tree matures. Quaking aspen is even more distinctive, with nearly circular, pointed leaves that tremble (or "quake") in the slightest breeze, creating a unique sound that when heard from a distance resembles running water. The greenish white bark often stands out in stark contrast to surrounding foliage (and even to the leaves on the tree) and frequently appears dotted or marked with dark patches, from wherever limbs have fallen or the tree has sustained an injury. In fall, when the leaves turn bright golden yellow before falling to earth, all of these unique splendors meld together to create a traditional Thanksgiving feast for the senses.

Habitat and Range: Moist woodlands and riparian areas throughout most of western North America. Black cottonwood primarily inhabits riverbanks and wet floodplains, up to about 5,000 feet. Quaking aspen is mainly an upland tree, growing in forest clearings up to timberline. All poplars require an ample and consistent water supply to survive. If surface water is not visible near one of these trees, you can assume that the roots are being fed by a subterranean water source.

Edibility: Although bitter, the catkins and leaf buds of all poplars are high in vitamin C and may be consumed when necessity outweighs their unpleasant flavor.

Medicinal Uses: All poplars contain varying amounts of salicin, the active ingredient in aspirin, and preparations of the leaves or inner bark (cambium) can be used to relieve pain, inflammation, and fever (just like aspirin). The sticky, reddish resin covering the young leaf buds in early spring is known by herbalists as balm of Gilead. The buds are plucked from the lower branches and soaked in alcohol (or another appropriate solvent) to release and thin the resin, which is then used to make infusions or salves. Balm of Gilead has been used for centuries as a broad-spectrum anti-inflammatory and vulnerary (to aid in the healing of wounds). It is also believed to have antioxidant qualities.

Black Cottonwood   *Populus trichocarpa*   Quaking Aspen   *Populus tremuloides*

Young leaf buds covered with sticky, red "balm of Gilead."

Prickly Lettuce
Lactuca serriola

Sunflower Family
Compositae

Prickly lettuce is characterized by spines lining the midribs and margins of its leaves, a trait that makes this plant easy to identify during all stages of its growth. The flowers are yellow and look like small dandelions. When mature, this multi-branched, 12- to 60-inch-tall annual or biennial weed has stem-clasping basal leaves that oddly twist upside-down to face the upper leaf surfaces toward the ground. The stems and leaves contain a sticky, white latex.

Blooms: May to July.

Habitat and Range: An import from Europe and now a common weed in gardens and disturbed sites across North America.

Edibility: The young leaves are edible, either raw or in salads, provided that their spines have not hardened with age. After the plant matures, its spines and bitter white latex make it unpalatable.

Medicinal Uses: Once known as lettuce opium, the latex of this plant possesses weak narcotic qualities. Although it is rarely used, herbalists know prickly lettuce as a safe and mild sleep aid and painkiller. Using the latex of this plant entails the tedious task of cutting the ⅛-inch-diameter stems and scraping the white fluid onto a surface where it can be dried. Whether this process is motivated by medicinal necessity or unrealistic recreational hopes, chances are good that any perceived needs will vanish days before anyone can collect a usable amount. The latex of this plant was once evaluated for use in manufacturing rubber products, but has since been deemed economically unfeasible.

Look-Alike Plants: Prickly lettuce is easily confused with dandelion and several other weedy, yellow-flowered composites. Remember *Lactuca serriola*'s prickly characteristics, and you will easily differentiate it from all others.

Prickly Lettuce   *Lactuca serriola*
Inset: The midrib spines make it an easy plant to recognize at any stage of growth.

Prickly-Pear Cactus
Opuntia species

Cactus Family
Cactaceae

Several *Opuntia* species are present in various habitats throughout the West. Those we know as prickly-pear cactus are remembered for their spiny, pear-shaped, yellow, orange, or bright red fruits. Variations in appearance between species include the size of the plant, the density of the spines, and the shape of the plant's fleshy segments, frequently referred to as paddles or beaver tails. For food or medicinal purposes, all are useful.

Blooms: Opportunistic, largely dependent on available moisture.

Habitat and Range: When we think "cactus," we usually think of the dry, hot desert. Members of this genus, however, are varied in their choice of habitat. The universal requirements for these species are a dry climate and gravelly soil, and if these are met, you can find a species of *Opuntia* just about anywhere in the western United States. In eastern Montana, Wyoming, and the high, cold deserts of eastern Nevada, temperatures frequently dip deep into subzero lows, but species such as *O. fragillis* can thrive beneath a blanket of snow.

Edibility: The succulent but seedy fruits of all species are edible, once the spines have been scorched or carefully peeled off with a sharp knife. The flavor ranges from bland to sour or sweet; at best, they taste like sweet pomegranates. The "paddles" of many of the southwestern species are delicious when peeled and eaten raw, cooked, pickled, or candied. Indian tribes of the Southwest often transplanted wild prickly-pears to cultivated plots, and many are still growing (visible in obvious crop rows) in the coastal canyons of southern California. Prickly-pear cactus is commercially grown and widely marketed in Mexico and the United States Southwest.

Medicinal Uses: Indians of the West Coast used preparations of prickly-pear to treat wounds, burns, contusions, warts, and even to facilitate childbirth. Modern herbalists recognize the plant's slippery-oily juice as a useful emollient and demulcent, which may be used externally to soothe dry, irritated skin or internally as a diuretic or anti-inflammatory agent for the digestive and urinary tracts. Recent scientific studies in Mexico suggest that the juice may be effective in lowering blood sugar in cases of juvenile-onset diabetes, particularly where chronic hyperglycemia prevails.

Prickly-Pear Cactus *Opuntia* species

Pyrola
Pyrola species

Heath Family
Ericaceae

Pyrola is frequently referred to as wintergreen because of its cold-hardy qualities. Provided you can find them, these perennial evergreens are often in choice condition throughout winter, even beneath a blanket of snow in subzero temperatures. *Pyrola asarifolia* (pink pyrola) is one of the largest (up to 12 inches) and most widespread pyrolas. Like many other broad-leafed species, it is characterized by nearly circular, glossy, dark green, petiolate leaves arranged in flattened, basal rosettes. Large groups of *P. asarifolia* commonly carpet the forest floor in densely spaced, ground-hugging colonies, the result of the plants' extensive rhizomes sending up shoots from the many nodes along their lengths. Flowers each have five petals and are borne on an erect, leafless stalk rising well above the rest of the plant. Although the flowers also distinguish the plant, they tend to bloom only a few at a time, often inconspicuously among other vegetation.

Blooms: June to August.

Habitat and Range: Pyrolas require a mysterious balance of fungi and other soil constituents to survive. They are most abundant in shaded, moist forests where dead wood and deep compost are plentiful, particularly where humankind has not encroached. Several species are widely distributed across the Northern Hemisphere.

Edibility: The leaves are edible but tend to be too tough, bitter, and astringent to enjoy.

Medicinal Uses: This plant has a long folkloric history as a broad-spectrum astringent. American Indians used various preparations of the plant to treat urinary diseases, mouth and throat inflammations, postpartum swelling, hemorrhoids, and insect bites, and also as a styptic agent to stop bleeding. Contemporary herbalists who care about the fate of their chosen medicines recognize pyrola as an excellent substitute for pipsissewa (*Chimaphila* species), another member of the heath family that is being overharvested as an ingredient in popular soft drinks.

Look-Alike Plants: Because of their woody stems and narrowly heart-shaped, often serrated leaves, some species such as *P. secunda* (one-sided pyrola) or *P. uniflora* (wood nymph) are sometimes mistaken for seedlings of the Rose or Poplar family. Once the central flower stalk of pyrola begins to develop, their true identity becomes obvious.

Pyrola *Pyrola asarifolia*

Raspberry
Rubus species

Rose Family
Rosaceae

Wild raspberries are generally categorized by color, red or black. Leaf and stem characteristics among members of this widespread genus of shrubs vary from species to species. At least twenty species of *Rubus* inhabit western North America. Most have pinnately divided leaves and five-petaled white flowers. They are generally found and remembered as tangled masses of thorny, trailing biennial stems that yield a tasty reward to anyone brave enough to reach the choicest berries. Although flavor quality and size varies between species, the fruits of all species look essentially the same as the cultivated, market varieties and, in most varieties, are borne from axillary or side-branch flowers. Thimbleberry *(Rubus parviflorus)* is the most unusual-looking member of the *Rubus* clan, with large (2- to 6-inch) lobed leaves that resemble those of a maple tree, no thorns, and terminal, main-stem clusters of two to three flowers or fruits.

Blooms: April through June.

Habitat and Range: The diversity of *Rubus* species and the number of roadside bramble patches progressively increases north through the Rocky Mountains or the coastal states of the West. In the Northwest, where many species are regarded as invasive weeds, *Rubus* is an abundant inhabitant of pastures, roadside ditches, and riparian habitats. Red raspberry *(Rubus idaeus)* is one of the most common species throughout the northern Rocky Mountains, inhabiting streambanks and moist hillsides up to timberline.

Edibility: Although flavor quality varies between species, most wild raspberries rate as good or better than their commercial counterparts. Thimbleberry ranks as my personal favorite (the fact that it has no thorns plays into this), but fruit yields of this species are always scant.

Medicinal Uses: The leaves and flowers of *Rubus* are high in vitamins and minerals and, when dried, make a delicious tea. Raspberry-leaf tea has long been regarded as a "female tonic," to nourish and strengthen the female reproductive organs. This is likely attributed to the plant's fragrene content, a substance believed to tone the body's smooth muscle organs.

> **WARNING! Raspberry leaves should only be used fresh or completely dried. During the wilting process, the leaves temporarily develop mildly toxic substances. Also, take into account the possible presence of an herbicide before eating berries, and avoid eating from roadside plants because of fuel residues.**

Red Raspberry *Rubus idaeus*

Thimbleberry *Rubus parviflorus*

Red Clover
Trifolium species

Pea Family
Leguminosae

Red clover was introduced from Europe for agricultural purposes, and escaping cultivation, it made itself at home across North America. It is characterized by the predominantly three-lobed leaves of the *Trifolium* genus, of which there are dozens of species and cultivars distributed throughout the West. The differences between these many choices may be minute, and positive identification of a specific *Trifolium* can be challenging. The identification of red clover can begin by recognizing its red, globe-shaped flowers and its softly hairy stems. Second, we can see that the flower stems (pedicels) are shorter than each of the leaf stems (petioles). And finally, red clover has a taproot, whereas many clovers have rhizomes. If all this fails to satisfy the question of identity, cheat—find some that has been cultivated and formulate some personalized notes for future reference.

Blooms: April to July.

Habitat and Range: Widespread in cultivated fields and gardens, along road margins, and in a variety of disturbed areas where the plant has largely been introduced through agricultural activities, throughout North America and much of the world.

Edibility: The entire plant is edible and nutritious. The dried flowers make an enjoyable tea.

Medicinal Uses: Red clover has long been regarded a traditional "blood purifier" by Chinese and Western herbalists. The term "blood purifier" refers to red clover's nutritive and tonic effects on the liver and its reputed ability to help the body eliminate waste materials from the blood. Red clover has been shown to contain coumarin compounds, which are known to thin the blood. Scientific evidence suggests that this herb may also possess antitumor qualities.

Red Osier Dogwood
Cornus stolonifera

Dogwood Family
Cornaceae

A spreading shrub or small tree, red osier is usually found growing in streamside thickets with an often dense assortment of willows, alders, and other water-loving flora. Named for the purplish red color of its twig bark, red osier usually stands out among its neighbors. Opposite leaves are ovate and pointed, up to 3 inches in diameter, with undersides that are finely haired and lighter in color than the topsides. Like other dogwoods (see bunchberry), red osier has deeply sunken, parallel leaf veins that exude a sticky latex. The fruits of this plant, too, are unique, appearing in terminate clusters of two-seeded, ¼-inch berries that are oddly bluish white.

Blooms: Late spring to early summer.

Habitat and Range: Moist, particularly riparian, soils, often in dense thickets throughout Alaska, Canada, and the mountains of the western and eastern United States.

Edibility: Although sometimes consumed by Indian tribes of the Northwest, the berries do not taste good and may be toxic if eaten in large enough quantities.

Medicinal Uses: The bark of this plant can be very laxative and was used by Blackfeet Indians for a variety of digestive disorders. Many North American tribes smoked the inner root bark as part of a ceremonial herb blend. In modern herbalism, the inner bark is used by advanced practitioners for its cornic acid content, a compound that is said to act as a "salicylate free" analgesic.

WARNING! All parts of red osier may be toxic, particularly if consumed in large quantities.

Red Clover   *Trifolium pratense*

Red Osier Dogwood   *Cornus stolonifera*

Strings of latex in the leaves of *Cornus* species.

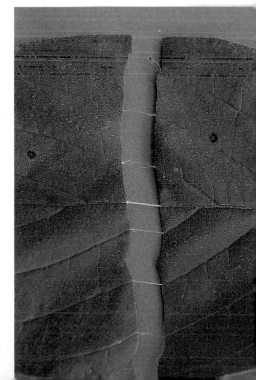

Red Root

Ceanothus velutinus

Buckthorn Family
Rhamnaceae

The *Ceanothus* genus comprises more than thirty species in western North America, and many of them cross-pollinate (hybridize), making identification difficult. The leaves of these hardy shrubs, though, offer a distinctive characteristic shared throughout the genus: each has three predominant veins extending from the leaf base to the outer margins of the leaf tips. The common name, red root, is attributed to the blood red color of the inner root bark. *Ceanothus velutinus* is one of the most common and widespread varieties in the West. The ovate leaves of this short (up to 5 feet) spreading shrub have shiny upper surfaces that feel gummy when pinched between your thumb and forefinger. The flowers are large, dense clusters of tiny greenish white blossoms that are sweetly fragrant—almost to the point of being nauseating (imagine the smell of boiling honey in an enclosed area). These shrubs play a critical role in the ecosystem as a consistent source of food and shelter. The seeds may lie dormant in the soil for two hundred years or more, or until a forest fire activates their germination.

Blooms: June to August.

Habitat and Range: Various species inhabit dry, sunny hillsides, from coastal shrub lands to open forest clearings, up to about 9,000 feet. *Ceanothus velutinus* is common and often profuse in the Rocky Mountains, from British Columbia south to Colorado, throughout the Cascades of Oregon and Washington, and in the coastal ranges of northern California.

Edibility: The dried leaves of many species of *Ceanothus* have long been recognized as a substitute for black tea. Otherwise, red root is best remembered as a medicine.

Medicinal Uses: Herbalists know red root as a "lymphatic stimulant and tonic." Chemical constituents in the leaves and root of this plant are believed to act to stimulate lymphatic circulation in areas of the body with lymphatic blockages or accumulations. With this in mind, red root is used in the treatment of ovarian cysts, fibroid tumors, tonsillitis, or any other area where lymphatic function is believed to be impaired. Native Americans and other early peoples sometimes chewed the leaves to relieve inflammations and irritations of the throat and mouth. Alkaloid constituents in the root of some varieties have been shown to lower blood pressure.

Red Root   *Ceanothus velutinus*

The distinctive leaf veins of *Ceanothus* species.

Sage
Salvia species

Mint Family
Labiatae

Wild sages are highly aromatic, smelling like the culinary variety *(Salvia officinalis)* but much stronger. The odor of sage is not entirely unique to *Salvia* species, however, and may be misleading unless other identifying characteristics are taken into account. Several species of wild sage share the unique "pebbled" leaf texture characteristic of their cultivated counterpart. The leaves and stems of many species are fuzzy, giving the plants a blue gray appearance. Flowers range from white to deep purple, depending on species, and are borne in whorled clusters where the leaves join the upper stem or in terminal racemes, again depending on species.

Blooms: Early to late spring.

Habitat and Range: Several species of sage inhabit the canyons and foothills of the western United States, with the greatest variety of native species in the Southwest. In the coastal canyons of southern California, species such as white sage *(S. apiana)*, black sage *(S. mellifera)*, Munz's sage *(S. munzii)*, and purple sage *(S. leucophylla)* often stand out as the predominant flora, growing in dense stands of 2- to 6-foot shrubs that may cover the landscape for miles. To the north or east, the distribution of *Salvia* species becomes more scattered and less varied, with plants generally smaller and less predominant in their habitat.

Edibility: If used in scant amounts, wild varieties of sage can be used in the same manner as the culinary varieties. It will impart a gamey flavor to foods, though, and many foraging gourmets find it unappealing.

Medicinal Uses: In traditional folkloric medicine, sage was used to wean infants. The mother would drink large amounts of the tea, and rinse her breasts with it as well. Modern herbalists recognize sage for its strong antimicrobial qualities, which are largely attributed to the plant's volatile oils. Sage tea is frequently used as a disinfectant mouthwash, an antiseptic skin rinse, and a douche. It is often found in commercial, over-the-counter preparations. Southwestern Indians used *S. apiana* as a soapless shampoo. The dried leaves and stems of the same variety are smudged (burned) in Native American ceremonies.

Look-Alike Plants: Several *Artemisia* species, such as wormwood *(A. vulgaris)* and sagebrush *(A. tridentata)* are typically mistaken for sage because of their similar aroma and often misleading common names. In fact, these plants are of the unrelated Sunflower family and are not edible. Confusion can be avoided by remembering that like other members of the Mint family, the leaves of sage are always opposite, whereas *Artemisia* species have alternate leaves.

White Sage   *Salvia apiana*

Munz's Sage flowers   *Salvia munzii*

Most sages have a distinctive leaf texture.

Saint John's Wort
Hypericum species

Saint John's Wort Family
Hypericaceae

Saint John's wort is a sturdy perennial weed distinguished by its yellow, five-petaled flowers, each with many stamens, and its small (up to ¾-inch long), narrowly lance-shaped to elliptical, opposite leaves. The flowers and leaves are covered with tiny, purplish black dots, each containing hypericin, a medicinally active compound that is often visible as a red stain on the skin after rubbing the foliage between your fingertips. The size of Saint John's wort varies between species, but all look similar. The largest and most widespread species, *Hypericum perforatum*, may reach 32 inches tall, whereas *H. anagalloides* (bog Saint John's wort), one of the smallest, grows in mats and seldom exceeds 4 inches.

Blooms: Sometimes referred to as Fourth of July flower, Saint John's wort usually blooms from early July through August.

Habitat and Range: Habitat varies according to species, but the larger species tend to prefer dry to moist, open hillsides up to about 6,000 feet, whereas higher elevations and wetter habitats tend to support the smaller species. In the Pacific Northwest, *H. perforatum* and *H. formosum* are common and often profuse on open rangelands at foothill elevations, where they are regarded as noxious weeds because of their alleged toxicity to livestock. Saint John's wort is a European import that now ranges throughout the Pacific and Rocky Mountain States.

Edibility: Not edible.

Medicinal Uses: Despite this plant's reputation as an enemy to the agricultural industry, it offers humanity a large measure of hope as a medicine. It has been used for centuries as a topical vulnerary in the treatment of external ulcers and wounds. Folkloric uses include the tea as a remedy for diarrhea, worms, dysentery, and bladder disease. Current clinical trials strongly suggest that Saint John's wort may be effective in treating chronic depression, and herbalists frequently use it to treat injuries and infections of the nervous system. Laboratory studies show that the active ingredients hypericin and pseudohypericin may be active against retro-viruses, and the plant is being scrutinized in AIDS research.

WARNING! Saint John's wort has caused rare cases of photosensitive reactions (severe sunburn) in livestock, particularly animals with light skin pigmentation. Although toxicity in humans has been limited to a few unconfirmed cases involving ingestion of very large quantities by extremely fair-skinned individuals, use caution and moderation with this plant.

Saint John's Wort *Hypericum perforatum*

Hypericin-containing glands on Saint John's Wort leaf.

Salal
Gaultheria species

Heath Family
Ericaceae

This attractive plant exhibits many of the characteristics typical of its Heath family relatives, such as kinnikinnick *(Arctostaphylos uva-ursi)* and pipsissewa *(Chimaphila* species), but in larger form. The 2- to 4-inch, ovate, thick and leathery leaves alternate on strong, creeping stems. Each leaf has a shiny, dark green upper surface and a lighter, rougher underside. The small urn-shaped, pink flowers (much like kinnikinnick) are borne in axillary or terminate racemes. These racemes eventually develop into clusters of juicy, purplish black berries, which set salal apart from most other members of the Heath family.

Blooms: April to July. Fruits ripen in fall.

Habitat and Range: Ranges through the coastal mountains of central California north into the Alaska Panhandle, and east through the western slopes of the Cascades in Oregon and Washington.

Edibility: The berries are a tart-sweet treat when eaten raw or made into jams, pies, or wine.

Medicinal Uses: This plant can be viewed as an all-purpose herbal astringent. American Indians chewed the leaves and applied them as a first aid remedy for burns, and used the leaf tea as a treatment for heartburn, coughs, and tuberculosis. Herbalists sometimes use salal to treat mild cases of bladder inflammation.

Salsify
Tragopogon species

Sunflower Family
Compositae

Also known as goatsbeard or oyster root, salsifys are taprooted biennials characterized by their flowers, leaves, and the milky juice in their foliage. The genus can be divided into two categories: those with yellow flowers, and those with purple flowers. Aside from color differences, all the species are similar in appearance. Solitary flowers are borne on top of hollow stems, with the uppermost portion of each stem distinctly swollen at the flower's base. The flowers have beaklike bracts that are often as long or longer than the narrow, daisylike rays. In fall, the flowers develop into 2- to 4-inch-wide globe-shaped, fluffy seed heads, which look like giant versions of those produced by dandelion. The leaves are long (up to 12 inches) and narrow (less than ½ inch wide). The well-defined taproot is proportionately long and parsniplike. Plants may reach 40 inches tall.

Blooms: April to July. The flowers open only during the first half of the day, then close in the afternoon. On cloudy days, they do not open at all.

Habitat and Range: These imports from Eurasia now occupy poor soils and disturbed areas across North America. In the West, *Tragopogon dubius* and *T. pratensis* are the most common and widespread species. Both have yellow flowers. Of the less common purple varieties, *T. porrifolius* is sporadically widespread across North America.

Edibility: Salsify was introduced onto this continent as a root vegetable. Purple-flowered varieties such as *T. porrifolius* are far more palatable than their yellow counterparts, with roots that taste like oysters when cooked—a trait responsible for the nonstandard common name, oyster root. The yellow varieties, although edible, tend to be strong, fibrous, and bitter. Properly cultivated and tended in deep soil, salsify roots from the garden are more enjoyable than those harvested from the wild.

Medicinal Uses: Although seldom employed by herbalists, the root is sometimes used as a remedy for upset stomach and other gastric disorders.

Salal   *Gaultheria shallon*

Yellow Salsify, or Oyster Root
Tragopogon dubius

Serviceberry
Amelanchier alnifolia

Rose Family
Rosaceae

This large deciduous shrub or small tree (up to 16 feet tall) is easily identified by its alternate, oval leaves and juicy, dark purple fruits. The leaves are toothed only toward their tips, with entire (not toothed) margins at their bases. The white to cream-colored flowers each have five lance-shaped petals and are presented in loosely arranged clusters of two or more at the leafy ends of the side branches. The purple fruits each contain two seeds and have waxy outer skins.

Blooms: April to June. Fruits begin to develop by midsummer.

Habitat and Range: Common in riparian habitats and on moist, wooded hillsides up to alpine elevations. From Alaska to California, and east throughout the Rocky Mountains and New Mexico.

Edibility: The ripe, juicy berries are mildly sweet and are excellent eaten raw or made into jams. American Indians often dried the berries for long-term storage or for use in pemmican, dried cakes that contained any variety of fruits, nuts, or meats and were often carried for nourishment when traveling.

Medicinal Uses: American Indians sometimes used the green inner bark (cambium) in anti-inflammatory eyewashes, eardrops, and to help stop excessive vaginal bleeding. Such applications can be attributed to the astringency of the plant's tannic acid content. The berries were sometimes used to treat constipation and various stomach disorders. The berry juice makes a lovely purple dye.

Sheep Sorrel
Rumex acetosella

Buckwheat Family
Polygonaceae

Sheep sorrel is an 8- to 12-inch perennial characterized by its 1- to 2-inch-long, distinctly arrow-shaped leaves. The flowers are small, bright red or rusty brown, and form spikelike terminal clusters typical of the *Rumex* genus (see yellow dock). This plant is a successful and persistent survivor, reproducing aggressively both from its seeds and from extensive rhizomes. It often grows in large, ground-covering colonies and is viewed as a troublesome weed by the agricultural community.

Blooms: Through the summer.

Habitat and Range: Any variety of disturbed areas, but particularly where soil acidity is slightly elevated. Originally imported from Europe and now widespread across the Northern Hemisphere.

Edibility: The leaves of this plant are tender, juicy, and have a lemony flavor. They are high in vitamins C, A, and beta-carotene, and are excellent when used to sharpen the flavor of salads and soups. This plant should be consumed in moderation, though, because excessive quantities may cause severe stomach upset.

Medicinal Uses: Herbalists use sheep sorrel, as they do many members of the *Rumex* clan, as a liver stimulant and blood alterative that is useful in treating skin disorders and various other metabolic imbalances. A poultice of the fresh leaves is said to be useful in treating skin cancer and tumors, and the tea has traditionally been used for inflammations, fevers, and to prevent scurvy. The highly astringent roots were used as a remedy for diarrhea and to slow excessive menstrual bleeding.

> **WARNING!** The sour flavor of sheep sorrel comes from oxalic acid, a compound that may cause gastrointestinal irritation if consumed in large enough quantities.

Serviceberry   *Amelanchier alnifolia*

Sheep Sorrel *Rumex acetosella*

The unique, arrow-shaped leaf of sheep sorrel, *Rumex acetosella*.

Skullcap
Scutellaria galericulata

Mint Family
Labiatae

Skullcaps are distinguished from other mints by their blue flowers, which are borne (in most species) from the upper leaf axils in symmetrically arranged sets of two or more. The flowers are two-lobed and tubular, with one lobe that forms an upper lip and one that forms a larger, apronlike lower lip. The lance-shaped, finely to coarsely toothed leaves are opposite (like all mints), with very short (almost absent) petioles. Like most mints, skullcap has distinctly four-sided (square) stems. Unlike many mints, skullcap has no distinctive odor. Several species of skullcap inhabit the West, many of which have been cultivated.

Blooms: June to August.

Habitat and Range: Consistently wet areas where there is an equal mix of sun and shade, often growing beneath willows, poplars, and other trees and shrubs of riparian thickets, generally at elevations below 4,000 feet. Widely distributed across Canada and the United States.

Edibility: Not recognized as edible.

Medicinal Uses: Herbalists regard skullcap as one of the most effective herbal sedatives available. Used primarily in acute or chronic cases of nervous tension or anxiety, its calming effects are said to be mild but reliable. It is also believed to help relieve pain from nerve-related injury or disease. Historically, it has been used to treat convulsions, epilepsy, multiple sclerosis, hysteria, and delirium tremens. The primary active constituent in skullcap is scutellarin, a flavonoid compound that has been shown to possess sedative and antispasmodic qualities.

Look-Alike Plants: Skullcap is sometimes confused with speedwell (*Veronica* species), a blue-flowered, water-loving plant that often shares the same habitat. The flowers are quite different in structure, but a better differentiating point to remember is skullcap's square (mintlike) stem; speedwell has round stems.

Shootingstar
Dodecatheon species

Primrose Family
Primulaceae

Named for and characterized by the unique appearance of their nodding flowers, shootingstars emerge with the first early spring perennials and are easy to recognize. The flowers are ½ to 1 inch long and range from light pink to deep purple, usually with yellow at the base of the petals. Each petal bends distinctly backward, giving the flower the appearance of a shooting star. Although some species may grow to as tall as 16 inches and produce dozens of flowers (*D. pulchellum*), most shootingstars range from 4 to 8 inches on average and produce one to five flowers per plant. The size and productivity of this genus mainly depends on such environmental variables as climate and availability of water and sunlight.

Blooms: March to July.

Habitat and Range: Moist meadows and clearings, from near sea level (*D. pulchellum*) up to 11,000 feet (*D. alpinum*), throughout most of western North America.

Edibility: All parts of this plant are edible. Although many people do not like the texture, the leaves have good flavor when eaten raw. The roots can be fire roasted but generally do not yield enough edible material to justify the death of these beautiful plants.

Medicinal Uses: Although seldom used by modern practitioners, the leaf tea was employed by some northwestern Indian tribes as a treatment for cold sores.

Skullcap   *Scutellaria galericulata*   Shootingstar   *Dodecatheon* species

Spring Beauty
Claytonia lanceolata

Purslane Family
Portulacaceae

One of the first mountain wildflowers to bloom after the snow melts, spring beauty is easy to recognize by its flowers and distinctive leaf characteristics. The white or pink flowers have five petals, which each bear distinctive pink to red veins. The basal pair of narrowly lance-shaped leaves are on proportionately long petioles and quickly die back as the upper parts of the plant develop, leaving each stem with only two opposite lance-shaped leaves. The stems are generally hairless and succulent, often with a reddish tint. The root consists of a fleshy taproot *(Claytonia megarhiza, C. bellidifolia)* or a small, nutlike corm *(C. lanceolata)*. Several species of *Claytonia* inhabit the West; all are small plants (usually shorter than 8 inches), and all are similar in appearance.

Blooms: Almost immediately following spring thaw.

Habitat and Range: Moist meadows and mountain slopes, from Alaska south to New Mexico and California.

Edibility: All parts of this plant are edible. The tender leaves and stems may be eaten as a salad green or used as an attractive garnish. The roots (or corms) have a slightly sweet, ricelike flavor, and are good when eaten raw or baked like miniature potatoes. Spring beauty often inhabits delicate soils, however, which may be particularly vulnerable to human impact, and the small plants usually do not yield enough food to justify their subsequent demise. In the interest of being conscientious, spring beauty is best remembered as a survival food.

Medicinal Uses: None known.

Spring Beauty   *Claytonia lanceolata*

Stonecrop
Sedum species

Stonecrop Family
Crassulaceae

Stonecrops are low-growing perennials with succulent stems and leaves. The leaves vary in size and shape between several species, but most are smaller than ½ inch long and either cylindrical *(Sedum stenopetalum)* or flat *(S. oregonense)* and lance shaped or oval. The flowers are white, red, purple, or, most commonly, yellow and are borne in flattened, terminate clusters on stalks rising above the rest of the plant. The roots are creeping rhizomes or stolons (roots that creep aboveground). Most of our stonecrops are small, mat-forming plants, seldom reaching 12 inches high. The Latin name *Sedum* is derived from *sedeo,* which means "to sit" in reference to the plant's squashed stature.

Blooms: April to July, depending on geographical niche and climatic variances.

Habitat and Range: As their common name implies, stonecrops like rocky soils. Aside from that, habitat varies among species. Look for them on talus slopes and rocky banks, from sea level to above timberline across North America. *Sedum stenopetalum* and the similar *S. lanceolatum* are found in predominantly dry, sunny locations at subalpine elevations from Alaska south to California and east throughout the Rocky Mountains and New Mexico. *Sedum oregonense* is common throughout the Cascades in Oregon.

Edibility: The entire plant is edible. The leaves have a bland, slightly cucumber-like flavor and are good in salads or eaten as a trail snack. The leaves of most high-altitude species stay green and juicy throughout winter, making it an important plant to remember for survival purposes. To find the plants in snow, look for the dried flower stalks rising above the surface of the snow. They are usually rust colored, with dried flowers that are distinctly star shaped and easy to recognize.

Medicinal Uses: Juicy, mucilaginous, and slightly astringent, this plant is useful as a soothing field remedy for minor burns, insect bites, and other skin irritations — simply squeeze the juice onto the affected area. American Indians used a decoction of the root for sore throats and eye irritations.

Wormleaf Stonecrop   *Sedum stenopetalum*

Creamy Stonecrop (with Wild Strawberry)   *Sedum oregonense*

Sweetroot
Osmorrhiza occidentalis

Parsley Family
Umbelliferae

Also known as western sweet Cicely, this 16- to 50-inch-tall plant offers the aspiring herbalist or wild foods enthusiast a safe introduction to the otherwise frightening Parsley family. Like other members of this large family, sweetroot presents its tiny flowers in terminal, umbrella-shaped inflorescences that do little to assure us that the plant is not the deadly water hemlock *(Cicuta douglasii)*. And the hollow stems, leaves, and roots also closely resemble those of water hemlock. The strong, aniselike pungency of *Osmorrhiza occidentalis* clearly differentiates it from all other Umbelliferaes, making positive identification safe and easy. Other species of sweetroot, such as the smaller (up to 36 inches) *O. chilensis* (mountain sweetroot), have little or no discernible odor but offer us fruit (seed) characteristics, definitive of the entire *Osmorrhiza* genus, to again make positive identification comfortably possible. The narrow, compressed, ¼- to 1-inch fruits of sweetroot point skyward, and when dry, they are hard and nearly black. Flowers of *O. occidentalis* are yellow, those of *O. chilensis* are greenish white.

Blooms: June to August.

Habitat and Range: Sunny, moist ravines, roadbanks, and the edges of riparian areas, but not in standing water. Mountainous areas up to about 6,000 feet, from British Columbia south into California and throughout the Rocky Mountain States.

Edibility: *O. occidentalis* has the same strong taste as its odor. The root bears the strongest flavor, somewhere between licorice candy and anise, and it quickly overpowers the taste buds. It is good, if used in small quantities, to sweeten herb teas that might otherwise be unpleasant. *Osmorrhiza chilensis* is mildly sweet and was often used by American Indians to flavor various foods.

Medicinal Uses: *Osmorrhiza occidentalis* is gaining popularity among herbalists. Clinical studies suggest that it may act to moderate blood sugar imbalances while inhibiting fungal reproduction in the body, making it potentially useful in the treatment of candidiasis and fungal infections of the digestive tract and reproductive systems. The root is also believed to stimulate mucous membranes in the intestinal tract, thus aiding in digestion. Other varieties of sweetroot (such as *O. chilensis*) are believed to be much weaker and are generally not used for medicinal purposes.

Look-Alike Plants: Sweetroot resembles the very poisonous water hemlock. If the plant smells strongly like anise, though, it is sweetroot. Water hemlock exhibits a unique leaf vein characteristic that singles it out from other Umbelliferaes. The smaller mountain sweetroot *(O. chilensis)* is sometimes confused with baneberry *(Actaea rubra)*, a toxic member of the Ranunculus family. Baneberry is easy to distinguish from mountain sweetroot by its terminal cluster of red or white berries. For more on water hemlock and baneberry, see Part II, Toxic Plants and Advanced Medicines.

Sweetroot, or Western Sweet Cicely
Osmorrhiza occidentalis

Mountain Sweetroot   *Osmorrhiza chilensis*

Thistle

Carduus, Silybum, or *Cirsium* species

Sunflower Family
Compositae

As you thumb through various plant keys and field guides, you quickly notice the common name "thistle" used generically for hundreds of sunflowers as a descriptive but not necessarily definitive term. In this profile, we will focus on musk thistle *(Carduus nutans)*, milk thistle *(Silybum marianum)*, and members of the *Cirsium* genus. The taxonomic differences between these three groups of thistles are often so minute that you wonder why botanists have chosen to group them separately. In essence, *Carduus* species have smaller but stiffer spines on their flowers than *Cirsium* and leaves that grow off the stems in a winged fashion. Milk thistle looks much the same but has a webbed pattern on its leaves. Otherwise, thistles are distinguished by their deeply lobed, alternate, often spiny leaves; their stout, often spiny stems; and their large (up to 2 inches wide) white to purple disk flowers, each resembling a miniature artichoke (another thistle).

Blooms: April to July (variable between species and depending on environment).

Habitat and Range: Many of our thistles are aliens, and in many areas of the West they are viewed as troublesome weeds. Look for them in pastures, cultivated fields, along the margins of roads, and in other disturbed sites across North America.

Edibility: I have confused you with three genera of plants in one profile because all of these thistles are edible, at least in small amounts. Palatability varies tremendously between species and even individual plants, but the peeled and cooked leaves or stems may be used as a potherb. Many are quite good, with a flavor typical of commercially produced artichokes, but most are tough and bitter and are best remembered only for survival purposes.

Medicinal Uses: Milk thistle *(Silybum marianum)* is well known for its tonic effects on the liver. The active compound silymarin is found in the seeds of the plant and has been shown to strengthen, protect, and regenerate liver cells in cases of chronic or acute liver damage. Other thistles have been used for centuries in the treatment of maladies ranging from stomachache to diabetes. American Indians used various species of *Cirsium* to treat respiratory congestion, dermatitis, parasitic infections, and venereal disease, and to help stop bleeding, stimulate milk production in nursing mothers, and even as a contraceptive.

WARNING! Some thistles contain potentially carcinogenic alkaloids. These plants should never be consumed in large quantities.

Bull Thistle *Cirsium vulgare*   Musk Thistle *Carduus nutans*

Twisted-Stalk
Streptopus amplexifolius

Lily Family
Liliaceae

Twisted-stalk is a creeping, forest floor perennial easily recognized by the unique-ness of its fruit and foliage. Alternate, egg-shaped to broadly lance-shaped leaves clasp and completely encircle the branched stems at their bases. Bell-shaped green or yellow flowers dangle from the upper leaf axils on small, wiry stalks that have a distinctive kink in them, giving each the twisted appearance that has earned the plant its common name. The flowers later develop into bright red, juicy, oval, ½-inch berries that boldly contrast with the surrounding foliage, making the plant easy to locate in even the thickest overgrowth.

Blooms: May to July. Fruits develop by late summer.

Habitat and Range: Shaded streambanks and moist thickets of the montane and subalpine zones across most of North America, excluding Mexico.

Edibility: Twisted-stalk is also known as wild cucumber, not because of any appar-ent resemblance it shares with a cucurbit but for the mildly sweet, cucumber-like flavor of its juicy ripe berries. They are excellent as a trail snack or in salads. Moderation is advised, however, because the berries are also known as "scoot berries" for their mild laxative effect when consumed in very large quantities. When positive identification can be accomplished, the tender, young shoots can be used as a salad green—they, too, taste like cucumber.

Medicinal Uses: Aside from being mildly laxative, the juice of the berries can be used to cool and soothe minor burns and skin irritations.

Look-Alike Plants: Twisted-stalk is frequently confused with false Solomon's seal, a lily that produces its flowers and fruits in a terminal inflorescence, unlike the axillary flowers and fruits of this plant (see false Solomon's seal). Young twisted-stalk closely resembles various other lilies, some of which are toxic. Remember to look for twisted-stalk's unique flowers and fruits.

> **WARNING! When young, twisted-stalk may be difficult to distinguish from other members of the Lily family, some of which are highly toxic (see false hellebore in Part II). For this reason it is best to limit your ingestion of twisted-stalk to the ripe berries.**

Twisted-Stalk   *Streptopus amplexifolius*

Usnea Lichen
Usnea species

Lichen Family
Parneliaceae

The plantlike result of a symbiotic association between algae and fungi, usnea lichen is an important and versatile natural medicine that demands a place in these pages. At least four species of *Usnea* are abundant throughout the western United States and Canada. They all look much alike and are generally seen clinging from the bark or limbs of dead or living trees. Commonly known as old man's beard, usnea is always light gray green; it does not change color throughout its life—the brown, yellow, red, or orange lichens seen growing beside usnea are of entirely different genuses (and there are thousands of species). Usnea is easily identified by pulling apart the outer sheath of its main stem. Inside, you will find a tiny *white* central cord much like an elastic thread. If the main stem is gray green throughout, it isn't usnea.

Habitat and Range: Forested areas of temperate North America.

Edibility: Although usnea is not edible, several species of lichen are, and I encourage anyone with an interest in developing good wilderness skills to learn about a few lichen species from a reputable source.

Medicinal Uses: I have included *Usnea* in this book because it has the potential of saving your life. The use of lichen as medicine dates back in recorded history to at least 1600 B.C., when it was used by Chinese, Greek, and (probably) Egyptian healers. Today, it is still used frequently in Chinese medicine (Sun Lo) to treat tuberculosis, and with the development of modern technologies, scientific studies have validated centuries of its use. Usnea extract has been shown to be effective against a wide spectrum of bacterial and fungal infections, and for this reason, it is a popular ingredient in many commercial preparations throughout Europe. Laboratory studies and clinical trials suggest that usnea may be more effective than penicillin in inhibiting the growth of gram-positive bacteria such as streptococcus, pneumococcus, and various strains of tuberculosis in the human body. It also has immunostimulant qualities, and the polysaccharide constituents in several species of *Usnea* have been shown to have antitumor effects in animals. In field emergencies where first aid equipment is not available, usnea lichen can be applied directly to an open wound, where it will serve as an antimicrobial compress to stop bleeding and prevent infection. Everyone who takes to the wilderness is well advised to put such valuable knowledge into the long-term memory bank.

Usnea Lichen   *Usnea* species

The white inner cord that differentiates usnea from other lichens.

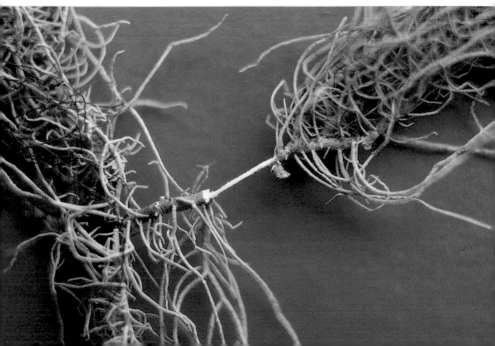

Valerian

Valeriana species

Many people relate the strongly aromatic roots of this plant to the odor of dirty gym socks. Although I once shared this universal opinion, I now relate valerian's odor to something unique and pleasantly earthy. Once you have smelled the odor of this plant, identification becomes as simple as dipping a finger into the soil to scratch a root. The foliage of valerian is unique, too. The plant first emerges as a cluster of loosely arranged lance-shaped leaves, which usually remain larger than the leaves of the mature upper plant. The upper leaves are opposite, pinnately divided, and become progressively smaller toward the top of the plant. The flowers are small, have three stamens (the pollen-bearing part), range in color from white to pink, and are borne in branched, terminate clusters. The roots are stringy, brown, and pungent. Several species of *Valeriana* grow throughout North America, with size the primary difference among species. Most of them are less than a foot high.

Blooms: April to July, depending on altitude and climate.

Habitat and Range: In soils that retain moisture well into summer, on north-facing banks or hillsides or in partially shaded soils high in organic matter.

Edibility: Although the leaves and roots of *Valeriana edulis* were cooked and consumed by Indian tribes of the Northwest, this plant is not very palatable. The flavor more or less matches its odor. In view of its medicinal actions, it stands to reason that ingestion of meal-sized quantities could cause stomach upset.

Medicinal Uses: Valerian is perhaps the best-known herbal sedative in the world. It has been used for hundreds of years as a safe remedy for stress-induced anxiety, muscle tension, and insomnia. Wild animals are believed to use it for similar purposes. The fabled Pied Piper was said to have valerian in his pockets—which is perhaps why the animals followed him. Valerian extracts and teas are widely available in the modern marketplace.

Sitka Valerian *Valeriana sitchensis*

Violet
Viola species

Violet Family
Violaceae

Violets are low-growing herbs that in most cases grow in small, inconspicuous clumps of broadly spade-shaped alternate leaves. As soon as they bloom, the flowers quickly identify this plant; each with five petals arranged as two upper, two lateral, and one lower petal that has a nectar-holding, backward-pointing spur at its base. Each flower has five stamens. Collectively, flowers in this genus look like colorful little faces, sharing the same characteristics as the garden-variety pansy *(Viola arvensis)* or Johnny-jump-up *(V. tricolor)*. Violaceae represents a large family, with approximately twenty-two genera and nine hundred species worldwide. More than thirty species grow in the Pacific Northwest alone. They are generally grouped into three categories: those with blue or violet flowers; those with mainly white flowers; and those with yellow flowers. In the Mountain and Pacific West, most varieties of *Viola* are on the shorter side of 12 inches high when fully mature, with flowers seldom more than ¾ inch long.

Blooms: April to June.

Habitat and Range: Moist soils in full or partial shade; wild or escaped from cultivation across most of North America.

Edibility: The flowers of all violets are edible and palatable, with a delicate sweetness and vibrant color that can turn an ordinary green salad into the talk of a party. Most wild varieties are small and too pretty to harm, but garden varieties lend themselves to this purpose well. Organically grown pansy and Johnny-jump-up flowers are now available in many produce markets that specialize in gourmet vegetables. For people who insist on eating wild varieties, beware . . . the flowers are safe to eat in reasonable quantity, but the leaves often contain considerable amounts of saponins, soaplike compounds that may cause digestive upset if consumed in large enough quantities.

Medicinal Uses: The leaves of violet are said to possess diuretic, expectorant, and laxative qualities (probably because of the saponin). Folkloric uses include this plant as a mild sedative and "blood purifier" (alterative), which aids the liver in eliminating excess waste compounds in the blood. It has also been used by some herbalists as a tumor-reducing agent. In large enough quantities, the roots act as an emetic and were used by American Indians to induce vomiting in cases of poisoning.

> **WARNING!** Violet leaves may be toxic if ingested in large quantities. Consumption of the roots may cause vomiting.

Western Violet *Viola adunca*

Round-Leaved Violet *Viola orbiculata*

Canada Violet *Viola canadensis*

Watercress

Rorippa nasturtium-aquaticum

Mustard Family
Cruciferae

The first point to consider when identifying watercress is habitat—watercress is always standing in fresh water. The mostly glabrous (hairless), petiolate leaves of this plant are oval shaped or pinnately divided, with narrow lateral lobes and a wider lobe at the tip of each leaf. The small, white to purplish white flowers are characteristically mustardlike and borne in clusters on terminal stalks that arise from the upper leaf axils, each with four petals. The fruits are linear, ½- to 1-inch-long capsules, each containing two rows of tiny seeds. The floating, trailing stems and foliage of watercress may grow to 32 inches long, but usually only the top 4 to 6 inches are visible above the water's surface. Several yellow-flowered varieties of *Rorippa* share similar appearances but generally are not found standing in water.

Blooms: April to July, depending on climate, and often continually through summer.
Habitat and Range: Standing or slow-moving fresh water, across North America.
Edibility: Excellent in salads, sandwiches, and gourmet soups and sauces. The flavor is like peppery lettuce. Gather watercress only from clean water, and then thoroughly wash the greens and allow them to dry before eating; this helps to eliminate any undesirable microorganisms (such as *giardia*) that may be living in the foliage. Yellow varieties of *Rorippa* are edible, too, but not as delicious as watercress.
Medicinal Uses: Watercress can be medicinally applied in the same manner as its family relatives (see wild mustards).

Waterleaf

Hydrophyllum capitatum

Waterleaf Family
Hydrophyllaceae

Waterleaf is named not for its environment nor the content of its foliage, but by the way it cradles water droplets on its leaves. Everything about this 5- to 15-inch-tall plant is unique. The white, lavender, or blue flowers have stamens that protrude beyond their corollas, giving them a fuzzy appearance. The few but large (up to 6 inches long) leaves are deeply divided (almost to the midrib) and extend well above the flowers; the flannel-like leaf surfaces make it possible for them to hold water droplets. The roots are in the form of a thick, short rhizome.

Blooms: One of the first flowers of early spring, waterleaf blooms along the fringes of snowfields, with glacier lilies and buttercups.
Habitat and Range: Moist forest clearings in sun or shade, from about 3,500 feet to near timberline. From southern British Columbia, east of the Cascades to central California, and east to Colorado.
Edibility: The leaves, stems, and flowers of waterleaf were an important early spring food for American Indians. Although the foliage may be eaten raw, it tends to have a flavor and texture you would expect from a piece of bitter-tasting flannel shirt. Cooking the greens improves palatability considerably.
Medicinal Uses: The large leaves can be applied to minor wounds as a protective field dressing and have a slightly astringent quality that makes them useful in poultice form for insect bites and other minor skin irritations.

Watercress *Rorippa nasturtium-aquaticum*

Ballhead Waterleaf *Hydrophyllum capitatum*

Wild Ginger

Asarum caudatum

Birthwort Family
Aristolochiaceae

Although this plant is completely unrelated to the gingerroot sold in the market, it smells nearly identical. The slightest disturbance of wild ginger foliage immediately releases a gingerlike aroma guaranteed to delight the nose. Wild ginger is a perennial herb that reproduces mainly from an extensive network of rhizomes, a characteristic that explains why you find dense colonies of the plants carpeting the forest floor. The 2- to 5-inch-wide, dark green, somewhat hairy leaves are broadly heart-shaped (nearly circular) and are presented on long (up to 8 inches) petioles that extend directly from the rootstocks. The brownish purple, 1- to 3-inch-wide flowers are well described as odd, with three lobes tapering and curling away from the rest of the flower like insect feelers. Because the solitary flowers are borne in the leaf axils, at ground level, they are almost invisible beneath the large leaves. *Asarum caudatum* represents the most widespread of the three species in the West, which all look and smell similar.

Wild ginger lives in delicate, pristine habitats that are progressively disappearing from our planet. Human feet often do more damage than human hands overharvesting in *Asarum*'s ancient home. So please refrain from indulging in this plant and instead rejoice in its beauty, while we still can. Use market gingerroot for your dietary and medicinal needs.

Blooms: May to July.

Habitat and Range: Strictly a dark forest plant, requiring deep forest compost and ample shade to survive; particularly common in old-growth cedar forests of the Northwest, where it plays a critical role in aerating easily compressed soils. From the mountains and rainforests of British Columbia south through similar habitats in Washington, Oregon, northern California, and the Idaho Panhandle.

Edibility: Wild ginger tastes like commercially available gingerroot, with the exception that the leaves are more strongly flavored than the roots.

Medicinal Uses: Like gingerroot, wild ginger is known to be a peripheral vasodilator and diaphoretic herbal medicine. Herbalists recognize these actions as useful in helping the body to eliminate excesses that are characterized by various forms of dermatitis, or by circulatory impairments of the skin. The leaf tea is also said to be useful in expelling intestinal gas and in relieving an upset stomach. In other words, this plant is used in exactly the same manner as gingerroot, a species far less sensitive to habitat disruption.

Wild Ginger   *Asarum caudatum*

Wild Ginger leaf   *Asarum caudatum*

Wild Mustards

Brassica nigra, Capsella bursa-pastoris,
and *Lepidium perfoliatum*

Mustard Family
Cruciferae

The Mustard family is large and variable but is generally distinguished by its flowers and fruits. Hybridization is common, particularly among members of the *Brassica* genus, often making species identification difficult. The ¼- to ½-inch flowers characteristically have four petals, four sepals, and six stamens, with the two outermost stamens shorter than the inner four. The fruits are two-celled, with two to several seeds, and range between round and linear in shape. Like the flowers, they are borne in terminate globe-shaped to elongated clusters, depending on genus and species. The leaves are characteristically alternate. Clasping pepperweed *(Lepidium perfoliatum)* is one of our most distinctive mustards, with the bases of its upper leaves uniquely surrounding its reddish brown, 6- to 18-inch stems. Fruits are in the form of round capsules with notched tips, each containing two small seeds. Shepherd's purse *(Capsella bursa-pastoris)* seldom reaches 20 inches high and is distinguished from other mustards by its heart-shaped seed capsules, which contain several (always more than two) tiny seeds each. Large, leafy mustards such as black mustard *(Brassica nigra)* may reach 4 feet high, and when young they look much like market varieties of mustard.

Blooms: April to July.

Habitat and Range: Many of our mustards have been introduced from Europe or Asia, and a few commercial varieties have escaped cultivation. These three species are widely distributed across North America, in cultivated fields and other disturbed areas.

Edibility: The seeds of all mustards can be dried or used fresh as a substitute for black pepper. The raw or cooked greens of young plants are highly nutritious, containing considerable amounts of trace minerals and vitamins A, B, and C. Palatability varies from species to species; at best, the flavor is much like commercially available strains of mustard greens, but stronger. Older plants tend to become bitter.

Medicinal Uses: The seeds of this plant family are known to stimulate the production of digestive juices in the stomach, thus aiding in the digestive process. The seeds are also used to make a traditional mustard plaster, a practice dating back many centuries that is still employed today; a pastelike poultice of the seeds is sandwiched between moistened sheets of flannel and applied to the chest area for relief of bronchial congestion. Results are said to be achieved through a profound, chemically initiated warming effect (which may cause blisters if left on the skin too long). Herbalists value the seeds of shepherd's purse for their diuretic actions and believe that the tea or tincture of the seeds may aid in the elimination of excess uric acid from the body. The seeds of shepherd's purse are also said to act as a blood coagulant and vasoconstrictor, making the plant useful in stopping internal or external bleeding.

> **WARNING! Ingestion of mustard seeds in large quantities may lead to irritation of the stomach lining. Take care when applying any mustard preparation to the skin, as blistering may result.**

Black Mustard   *Brassica nigra*

Clasping Pepperweed   *Lepidium perfoliatum*

The flowers of black mustard, typical of most mustards, may vary in color.

Shepherd's Purse, *Capsella bursa-pastoris*. Each two-celled capsule contains several tiny seeds.

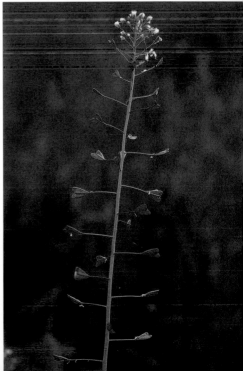

Wild Onion

Allium species

This large genus of perennial herbs is characterized throughout its ranks by a distinctive, onionlike odor. The leaves are slender and flat or cylindrical (often grasslike), extending directly from the bulb or thick rhizomes like the typical market varieties of garlic or onion. The flowers are borne on leafless, central stalks that rise above the rest of the plant in globe- or umbrella-shaped inflorescences.

Blooms: April to June.

Habitat and Range: Habitat varies with species, but dozens of varieties grow in open forest clearings and grasslands at foothill to subalpine elevations across most of the United States and Canada.

Edibility: Like their domesticated counterparts, wild onions are entirely edible. Their flavor is generally mild, with some species tasting like garlic and others like shallots. They are excellent as a trail snack or in any variety of cuisine that calls for onion or garlic.

Medicinal Uses: Onions have been used as medicine for centuries. Herbalists recognize their antiseptic, diuretic, expectorant, and carminative qualities. American Indians used various species of *Allium* in a wide range of remedial applications, from the simple care of cuts and burns to the treatment of male impotency. Like cultivated varieties of garlic, frequent doses of wild onions in the diet have been scientifically shown to reduce cholesterol levels in the bloodstream.

Look-Alike Plants: Wild onions can be confused with death camas (*Zigadenus* species), a highly toxic lily that shares the same habitat and a similar appearance. Wild onion is easy to differentiate from this toxic cousin by its distinctive onionlike odor. If it doesn't smell like an onion, do not eat it.

> **WARNING!** See death camas in Part II, Toxic Plants and Advanced Medicines.

Nodding Onion   *Allium cernuum*

The delicious bulb of wild onion.

Wild Rose

Rosa species

Rose Family
Rosaceae

Wild roses look and smell like their domesticated counterparts, with the exception that they have smaller flowers and leaves. Characterized by pink, five-petaled flowers, thorny stems, and bright red to purplish fruits (rose hips), this plant provides a safe, easy-to-identify, sensually delightful introduction to nature's pantry and apothecary.

Blooms: April to July.

Habitat and Range: Prefers consistently moist soils and commonly grows in dense thickets at road margins, irrigation ditches, and, especially, as the defensive edge of riparian habitats, up to about 6,000 feet. Several species are native across North America. *Rosa woodsii* (Wood's rose) represents one of the most widespread species of the West.

Edibility: The ripe "hips" are very high in vitamin C and are delicious when made into jelly or used as an herbal tea; they also make an excellent wine. Although edible and quite tasty if eaten raw, they tend to be too seedy for most palates.

Medicinal Uses: When we think of roses as medicine, we tend to recall reading "Vitamin C with Rose Hips" on bottle labels at the drugstore. The nutritive value of rose hips constitutes only a small fraction of the healing attributes this plant has to offer. American Indians used all parts of *Rosa* species in a wide variety of applications. The seeds were cooked and ingested for relief from muscular pains. The roots were used as a general-purpose astringent for diarrhea, sore throat, and conjunctivitis, and to stop bleeding. The flower petals were employed as a bacteriostatic, protective bandage on burns and minor wounds, and as a treatment for colic and heartburn. A poultice of the leaves was used for insect stings and bites, and folkloric accounts claim that rose-petal wine is useful for easing labor pains.

Wild Strawberry

Fragaria species

Rose Family
Rosaceae

Anyone familiar with a garden-variety strawberry plant will easily identify wild strawberry, which looks essentially the same but smaller. The elliptical or egg-shaped, coarsely toothed leaves are divided into groups of three leaflets and are clustered toward the bases of the stems. The flowers are white with five petals, five sepals, and stamens comprising brownish yellow centers. The red, juicy fruits are what you would expect pea-sized strawberries to look like. Wild strawberries are perennial creepers that take root from several nodes along their stems (also like their domesticated cousins). The seeds are distributed mainly through the droppings of various animals that eat the fruit.

Blooms: April to June, shortly after the spring thaw.

Habitat and Range: Forest clearings in well-drained, rich soils, from near sea level to subalpine elevations across most of the United States and Canada.

Edibility: Provided you can find them before every other creature in the forest does, the tiny berries are sweet and delicious. The dried leaves and flowers make an enjoyable tea.

Medicinal Uses: Strawberry-leaf tea is high in vitamin C and is known to possess diuretic and mild astringent qualities. Herbalists also regard the leaf tea as a tonic for the female reproductive system, using it in exactly the same applications as raspberry. The leaf tea is used to soothe inflammations of the mouth, eyes (conjunctivitis), and skin, and if used in large enough quantities, it is said to help relieve hay fever symptoms. The root is a stronger astringent medicine than the leaves, and is sometimes used as a remedy for diarrhea and other digestive disorders. Cree Indians called it *otehimika* and combined it with yarrow tea to treat insanity.

Wood's Rose   *Rosa woodsii*

Blueleaf, or Virginia Strawberry   *Fragaria virginiana*

Willow
Salix species

Willow Family
Salicaceae

Salix is a huge and widely varied genus of deciduous shrubs and trees. Describing the variables—and the hybridization possibilities—between the hundred or more species that inhabit temperate North America is impossible within the confines of this book. To serve as an introduction, though, we can examine the features typical throughout this broad range of possibilities. All willows are characterized by their flowers (or "catkins") and the distinctive nature of their leaf buds. The catkins are borne along the sides of the young twigs and side branches in early spring. Male and female catkins are borne on separate plants. The catkins first appear as silvery white fluffs of fur, a characteristic that has earned them the common name "pussy willows." This stage is brief, as they take on a more bristled, woolly, worm-like appearance as they develop into their sexual maturity. The leaf buds are sheathed by a single, smooth, brownish scale that looks much like the scale on a kernel of popcorn. This scale often remains attached until the flowers have fallen off and the leaves are nearly mature. The young leaf shoots each have a small winglike appendage at their base.

Blooms: Early spring, often long before the ground thaws in montane habitats.

Habitat and Range: Typically found near water or in soils that hold moisture for long periods of time (areas with a high clay content, for example). Aside from these guidelines, habitat varies widely between low desert and alpine elevations, throughout North America. To become familiar with willows, select a field guide specific to your locale, then begin looking along rivers and streams.

Edibility: The young leaves and the inner bark (cambium) are adequate as survival food, but taste bitter.

Medicinal Uses: Willow contains salicylates, compounds similar to those found in aspirin. In fact, willow bark is believed by many herbalists to be the precursor to this widely used analgesic drug. The entire plant contains the painkilling constituents; the highest concentrations are in the inner bark (cambium). Used in teas, the bark will act to relieve pain, reduce inflammation, and help lower fevers—like aspirin, although not as strong. The leaves or cambium, or both, may also be made into a poultice and used topically to relieve painful insect bites, minor burns, and other superficial skin irritations.

> **WARNING!** People who are sensitive to aspirin should not ingest any form of willow. Ingestion of large quantities may irritate the stomach lining.

Willow catkins, or pussy willows   *Salix* species

The scalelike leaf bud sheaths
of *Salix* species.

Salix geyeriana. Note the appendages at
the base of the leaves.

Yampa
Perideridia gairdneri

Parsley Family
Umbelliferae

Like most members of its family, yampa's white flowers are borne in umbels at the top of the plant, but the leaves, stems, and roots set it apart from its relatives. The single, wiry stem of this 1- to 3-foot-tall plant is often obscured by surrounding grasses, making it difficult to locate until the plant blooms. Once you locate the flower, examine the linear, 1- to 6-inch leaves, which are each divided into three to seven threadlike segments. Then, by carefully digging around the base of the plant, complete your investigation by viewing the small, oblong root, which looks like a shelled peanut.

Blooms: May to July.
Habitat and Range: Moist, open meadows and hillsides, up to about 7,500 feet, throughout most mountainous regions of western North America, excluding Mexico.
Edibility: The nutlike roots are crunchy and mildly sweet, with a flavor similar to water chestnuts, and they are excellent baked or steamed. Yampa was prized by American Indians, who harvested it to near extinction in many areas of the West. The seeds may be used as seasoning, substituting for yampa's relative, caraway. Yampa's scarcity in many areas, though, and its small food yield, make it difficult to justify its harvest and subsequent demise.
Medicinal Uses: Yampa was a popular Blackfeet Indian medicine. They used the root tea as a diuretic, laxative, expectorant, and to soothe a sore throat. The root was said to improve the endurance of their hunters and message runners and was sometimes fed to horses to give them more energy. This stands to reason, as the roots are believed to contain a considerable amount of rapidly assimilable carbohydrates.

Yarrow
Achillea millefolium

Sunflower Family
Compositae

Yarrow is characterized by its flat-topped terminal clusters of small, white to pinkish white flowers and its alternate, finely dissected, feathery leaves (*millefolium* means "thousand-leafed"). The entire plant is strongly aromatic, with a pungency similar to mothballs. The stems are typically woolly-hairy. Several cultivars of yarrow have been developed for the floral industry, and others have escaped cultivation in many areas. These plants are usually not as cold hardy as their wild cousins, and can be identified by their yellow, red, or peach-colored flowers.

Blooms: Beginning in May, and often lasting through the summer.
Habitat and Range: Throughout the Northern Hemisphere, from sea level to above timberline. The density of yarrow populations increases to the north through the western United States.
Edibility: Not recognized as edible—it is too bitter.
Medicinal Uses: Yarrow is one of the oldest and best-known herbal medicines still in use worldwide. The dried flowers and leaves are most frequently used as an ingredient in various cold remedies, where yarrow is believed to act as an expectorant and analgesic, and to promote sweating (a diaphoretic). It is also said to act as a vascular tonic that may be useful for varicosity and various other circulatory diseases. The fresh leaves may also be rubbed onto the skin as a temporary but effective insect repellent.

> **WARNING! Yarrow may cause dermatitis when applied to the skin of sensitive individuals. This plant contains thujone, a substance that may be toxic if consumed in large quantities over an extended period of time.**

Yampa   *Perideridia gairdneri*   Yampa's nutlike root *Perideridia gairdneri*

Yarrow   *Achillea millefolium*

Yellow Bells

Lily Family
Fritillaria pudica · Liliaceae

Yellow bells is a perennial with a simple, erect stem and narrowly lance-shaped (nearly grasslike) leaves that may reach as high as the entire plant. The plants are 4 to 12 inches tall and commonly produce a total of only two opposite leaves; when more than two leaves are produced, they are arranged alternately. As the common name implies, the nodding flowers are yellow and bell shaped. The plants bear one to three flowers, each with six stamens (the pollen-bearing part) and six petal-like segments. The scaly bulb is surrounded by several ricelike bulblets.

Blooms: March to May.

Habitat and Range: Open woods and grasslands, up to about 6,000 feet, from British Columbia and Alberta south to northern California, western North Dakota, Montana, Idaho, Wyoming, and Utah.

Edibility: The bulbs are edible and tasty, either raw or lightly cooked. Dozens of these beautiful plants, though, would have to die to make a meal-sized portion. Aside from absolute necessity, the plant's relatively low food value cannot justify such a harsh impact.

Look-Alike Plants: Many members of the Lily family share a close resemblance when young, and some are very toxic. Positive identification may be difficult unless this plant is in full bloom.

Yellow Dock

Buckwheat Family
Rumex crispus · Polygonaceae

Yellow dock is a hearty, taprooted perennial that may grow to 5 feet high. The elongated (up to 12 inches long and 4 inches wide), lance-shaped, basal leaves are borne on proportionately long petioles and are often curled at their margins. The alternate stem leaves are smaller but more numerous. The single, stout stem is commonly red and bears long, terminate clusters of small, greenish white flowers above the rest of the plant. As the flowers mature and dry, they turn rusty red and often stand out in bold contrast to the surrounding flora. Of the twenty-five or more species of *Rumex* that inhabit North America, yellow dock (*Rumex crispus*) is representative of the larger members of its genus. Of the larger species, some are taller plants (*R. occidentalis*), smaller plants (*R. venosus*), have broader leaves (*R. obtusifolius*), or smaller leaves (*R. sangineus*) than yellow dock, but all are essentially similar in overall appearance and usefulness. At the smaller end of the genus, species such as sheep sorrel (*R. acetosella*) look different and vary in their usefulness.

Blooms: May to July.

Habitat and Range: Widely distributed in disturbed areas across North America. The entire *Rumex* genus is imported from Europe.

Edibility: The young leaves of yellow dock and similar species are high in iron and vitamins, and if cooked in two or more changes of water, they can be enjoyable (if consumed in moderation). The entire plant is tart, as it contains considerable amounts of oxalic acid, a compound to avoid in large quantities.

Medicinal Uses: Yellow dock has long been regarded by herbalists as a liver stimulant and blood purifier. Its primary use is to stimulate biliary function and to aid in reestablishing metabolic balances in the liver and digestive tract. Some people believe that preparations of the root, taken internally, will help the body in eliminating concentrations of lead, arsenic, and other heavy metals.

WARNING! Yellow dock contains considerable amounts of oxalic and tannic acids. Although oxalic acid is also present in spinach and beets, it can be toxic, causing severe digestive tract irritation if consumed in large enough quantities; the first symptom is mild nausea. Tannic acid, another common food plant constituent, can be irritating to the urinary tract and kidneys if consumed in high enough concentrations. The watchword here, as always, is moderation.

Yellow Bells *Fritillaria pudica*   Yellow Dock, or Curly Dock *Rumex crispus*

Yerba Santa
Eriodictyon crassifolium

Waterleaf Family
Hydrophyllaceae

The conspicuous yerba santa is often seen standing above the sages, buckwheats, and various other shrubs of its brushland habitat. It is a rather spindly plant, with leaves generously spaced along resilient stems that sway in the slightest breeze. This genus is characterized by its distinctly veined, lance-shaped, toothed alternate leaves and its tubular blue flowers, which are borne on short peduncles in loosely arranged terminal clusters. You can distinguish individual species of yerba santa by the unique appearance and texture of their leaves and stems. *Eriodictyon crassifolium* (woolly yerba santa) has leaves and stems covered with a distinctive soft fuzz, a trait that gives the entire plant a gray green, dusty appearance. *Eriodictyon trichocalyx* closely resembles *E. crassifolium* but is not as fuzzy. *Eriodictyon californicum* and *E. angustifolium* have darker foliage, which looks and feels as if it has been sprayed with sticky oil. The plants are pleasantly aromatic, with a sweet sagelike odor.

Blooms: March to June.

Habitat and Range: Coastal canyons and mountain slopes up to about 5,500 feet, from Baja California north to northern California and east to the western slopes of the Sierra Nevada, where it grows only sporadically. Yerba santa is conspicuously abundant along the highways of southern and central California.

Edibility: The leaves may be chewed as a trail substitute for chewing gum.

Medicinal Uses: Once listed as an official drug plant in America, contemporary herbalists still regard yerba santa as one of the best expectorants and decongestants available. The leaf tea or extract is said to be especially useful in "drying up" the excessive, watery mucus secretions that are associated with bronchial inflammations. American Indians used the plant for similar purposes.

Woolly Yerba Santa   *Eriodictyon crassifolium*

Yucca
Yucca species

Lily Family
Liliaceae

The various species of yucca are easy to recognize by their 1- to 4-foot-long, sword-like, spine-tipped leaves, which grow directly off a branched or unbranched trunk. Yucca bears fleshy, cream-colored, bell-shaped, distinctly lilylike flowers in clusters on terminal stalks. The large, succulent, podlike fruits contain black seeds.

Blooms: Yuccas bloom opportunistically according to periods of precipitation. They will often go without flowering during dry years.

Habitat and Range: Several species of yucca grow throughout the West, with their habitat varied between the coastal foothills and canyons of Baja and southern California (*Yucca schidigera*, Mojave yucca); the deserts of California, Arizona, New Mexico, Colorado, and Nevada (*Y. schidigera*, and *Y. baccata*, blue yucca); and the plains and high desert plateaus of Idaho, Montana, Wyoming, and the Dakotas (*Y. glauca*, soapwell yucca). In the deserts of the United States Southwest, Joshua tree (*Y. brevifolia*) commonly predominates as the tallest member of the high desert flora (up to 35 feet tall). The universal requirement for yuccas—even more important than hot weather—is low precipitation.

Edibility: Yuccas were important to Native Americans, who used them for food, as basketry and cordage materials (the leaves), and to make soap and medicine (the roots). The flowers of all species are edible and have a delicate, sweet flavor and juicy tenderness that brings the root vegetable jicama to mind. The seed pods, while still immature and juicy, were gathered by Indians and then peeled and baked, or sliced and dried for later use. The young flower stalks may be peeled and steamed as you would cook carrots.

Medicinal Uses: American Indians used yucca root in a wide assortment of medicinal applications. A decoction was used internally to treat various forms of digestive irritation and arthritis. In topical applications, it was used to rid the body of lice and to reduce hair loss. Blackfeet Indians used the steamed root poultice as a topical anti-inflammatory for bruises, sprains, and bone fractures. Today, yucca is popular among herbalists as an anti-inflammatory medicine believed to be useful in the treatment of joint injuries and rheumatoid conditions. Studies have shown that the root may be useful in treating inflammatory diseases of the urinary tract and prostate.

> **WARNING! Yucca contains saponins and other compounds that may cause nausea and vomiting if consumed in large quantities, especially when eaten raw.**

Mojave Yucca   *Yucca schidigera*

Joshua Tree   *Yucca brevifolia*

Part II

Toxic Plants and Advanced Medicines

The determining factor in whether a substance is poisonous is relative to the body's natural ability to absorb or eliminate it. In most cases, a general rule of moderation applies: if the body receives *anything* in quantities that it cannot effectively metabolize, an imbalance results, called toxicity. Most of us have tested this rule with one too many beers, our holiday assaults on the gastrointestinal tract, or perhaps a chronic and continuous ingestion of coffee. Each of these excesses amounts to a systemic overload and adds up to a low-level poisoning or worse.

Some plants, however, cannot be metabolized in any detectable amount without exacting a pricey toll on the body. These plants contain potentially toxic compounds in concentrations greater than moderation can govern, or they contain constituents that are antagonistic to our chemistry, causing structural damage or triggering systemic dysfunction. In these cases, the liver, kidneys, and other filtering mechanisms of the body become overloaded or are bypassed. Normal body function is impaired, and a poisoning results.

This is not to say that plant toxicity is insurmountable by science. Many plants that are poisonous in their whole form contain compounds or single elements that can be exploited for medicinal purposes. Black henbane or jimson weed, for example, are two very nasty nightshades that, although dangerous, contain alkaloid constituents that can be isolated from the rest of the plant to produce lifesaving drugs. Scientific methods of reduction accomplish this, removing a single plant constituent from perhaps thousands of others through exacting, modern technologies. Using poisonous plants as medicine is not exclusive to modern science. For hundreds of years, even the deadliest plants have been used in homeopathy, a modality of healing now making a comeback as an alternative to mainstream therapies. Founded by Samuel Hahnemann in the late 1700s, homeopathy was in the limelight of Western medicine until the advent of antibiotics and vaccines. It is a science that requires a precise understanding of human symptomology. After meticulous diagnostic investigation, a remedy is tailored to the specific needs of the individual, using plant, animal, or mineral compounds diluted from their original strength hundreds or even thousands of times. The goal of homeopathic medicine is to effect a desired physical or psychological response by stimulating body systems at very low, perhaps even molecular, levels. Most of the plants described in this book, poisonous or otherwise, are used in this way in homeopathic medicines. Even water hemlock, the deadliest plant in North America, has been proven as a homeopathic remedy, in scant concentrations that may be completely undetectable by laboratory analysis. Modern scientists are baffled by the effectiveness of this rapidly reemerging method of healing. Millions of people claim superior results from homeopathic therapies.

In this section, I have included descriptions of a small selection of very poisonous plants. Also described are some plants not generally considered toxic but which demand an added degree of respect or consideration in determining their identity (stinging nettle, for example). Many useful plants require scrupulous attention to their minute physical details to distinguish them from potentially harmful look-alikes. These details often are so minute or confusing to the novice that a strong measure of intimate familiarity is required—common sense is not enough. Examples of such plants include biscuitroot, osha, and angelica—three useful umbels that can be extremely difficult to differentiate from their poisonous cousins water hemlock and hemlock parsley.

As you read each of the following plant profiles, bear in mind that the natural roles of these plants and the potential benefits they hold are still largely undiscovered by science. We have only viewed these plants, like most aspects of nature, with the perceptions and preconceptions of a curious and worried child. We are only scratching the surface of possibility as we pick up where our ancestors left off several generations ago. Any one of these plants may contain great hope for the future of humanity. By acknowledging the tremendous possibilities that exist, the curious child can grow toward an earth-conscious level of awareness that addresses our health, not just our fear.

Angelica
Angelica species

Parsley Family
Umbelliferae

This hollow-stemmed perennial bears the typical characteristics of the Parsley-Umbel family. The flowers consist of umbrella-shaped clusters of tiny white blossoms arranged in a concentric inflorescence like the pattern of a fireworks burst. After blooming in fall, the umbels develop corky, tan-colored seeds that have a unique "winged" appearance, which serves as a memorable reference for the plant enthusiast: you can associate "angel wings" with "Angelica." This reference is very important, because angelica closely resembles an extremely poisonous look-alike, water hemlock *(Cicuta douglasii)*. Early in the plant's growth, positive identification can be confirmed only through leaf vein characteristics. The leaf edges of angelica are serrate and pinnately divided into opposing pairs, like water hemlock, except that the leaf veins extend from the midribs to the outer tips of the serrations. Water hemlock has leaf veins terminating *within* the notches of the serrations (see water hemlock).

Angelica has a distinctive "spicy celery" odor (particularly when bruised), which becomes increasingly recognizable as you become familiar with the plant. The large, tan-skinned root of the mature plant is well-defined as a taproot (carrotlike).

Blooms: June to August.

Habitat and Range: Several species of angelica grow in consistently moist meadows and along streambanks across the northern two-thirds of North America. The plant becomes less common to the south.

Edibility: An ingredient in gin and other liqueurs, the leaves of angelica are edible, with a strong but pleasant flavor similar to its cousin, lovage. They can be added to soups or stews but are generally too strong for raw consumption. The root is particularly strong and may be toxic if ingested fresh.

Medicinal Uses: Angelica has a long and well-defined history as a medicine. In China, *Angelica sinensis* is prepared as *dong quai*, an ancient antispasmodic medicine still in use to relieve cramping and other disorders of the digestive tract and female reproductive system. Western herbalists use this plant in similar applications, frequently in the treatment of menstrual disorders and menopausal discomforts.

Look-Alike Plants: Poisonous water hemlock.

WARNING! Although angelica is useful as a food and medicine, it may be difficult to distinguish from water hemlock, unquestionably the most poisonous plant in North America (one-quarter teaspoon of the root may be fatal within 15 minutes). Positive identification is essential and must be established through leaf or seed examination. Although many field guides claim that water hemlock can be distinguished by the presence of purple splotches or chambered roots, these guidelines are not always accurate and should not be used for identification purposes.

Angelica *Angelica* species

Angelica's unique leaf veins, which extend from the midrib to the outer tips of the serrations. Inset: Angelica seeds, *Angelica* species

Arnica

Arnica species

Sunflower Family

Compositae

Arnica is a large and diverse genus of species that often hybridize and can be confusing to identify. Two species *(A. cordifolia* and *A. latifolia)* predominate in western North America and embody characteristics that can be used to identify several other *Arnica* species. This plant has long, horizontal root systems (rhizomes) that send up shoots from several nodes to create sometimes profuse colonies of 6- to 12-inch-high plants. Arnica is a perennial that blooms during its second year of growth and every year thereafter. The bright yellow, 1- to 4-inch-diameter flowers are characteristic of sunflowers. The number of flower heads ranges from one to twelve per plant, depending on species and environmental conditions. The leaves are opposite, often downy in texture, and range from lanceolate *(A. latifolia)* to broadly heart shaped *(A. cordifolia)*, with the basal leaves larger than on the upper plant.

Arnica has a distinctive pine-sage odor, especially evident when the leaves of the mature plants are rubbed or bruised.

Blooms: May to July, depending on climatic variances and ecological niche.

Habitat and Range: Forest clearings and montane meadows, from the high mountains of southern California north to Alaska, and east into the Rocky Mountains of Colorado, Idaho, Wyoming, and Montana.

Toxicity: Although generally safe when used in topical applications, this plant may cause severe gastroenteritis if ingested.

Medicinal Uses: Many of us who have used a muscle liniment for strains, sprains, and bruises have used a product made from this plant. Herbalists and many health care practitioners maintain that the volatile oils of this plant can be absorbed through the skin to aid in the transport of blood accumulations and other fluids through a dilating action of subcutaneous capillaries. Commercial arnica preparations are frequently used by athletes.

> **WARNING!** Unless used in homeopathic doses, arnica can be highly toxic if ingested. This plant (and preparations of this plant) should only be used topically.

Heart-Leaf Arnica   *Arnica cordifolia*

Baneberry

Actaea rubra

Buttercup Family
Ranunculaceae

Baneberry is an erect perennial that may grow to 40 inches tall. The sharply toothed, lance-shaped leaves have long petioles and are divided into two to three segments. The plant bears several small white flowers in a dense, hemispheric cluster that later develop into slightly flattened, shiny, red or white ¼-inch berries. The entire plant is slightly hairy.

Blooms: Late spring to early summer. Fruits are usually present from August until the first or second hard frost.

Habitat and Range: Moist mountain forests and riparian habitats, always in at least partial shade, from the mountains of California north to Alaska and east throughout much of the forested areas of North America.

Toxicity: The entire plant is toxic if consumed as a food; the berries are the most poisonous part of the plant.

Medicinal Uses: Although this plant should be handled with extreme care, some advanced clinical herbalists find it useful as a strong antispasmodic. Within that professional circle, the root of baneberry is often regarded as a strong alternative to black cohosh *(Cimicifuga elata)*, an herb with a longstanding reputation as a remedy for menstrual cramping and menopausal discomforts.

Look-Alike Plants: Baneberry is sometimes confused with *Osmorrhiza chilensis* (mountain sweetroot), an edible member of the Umbel family that often shares the same habitat and a similar appearance. The most definitive distinguishing factor between baneberry and sweetroot is sweetroot's distinctive odor (see sweetroot).

> **WARNING!** Baneberry may cause cardiac arrest if consumed in large enough quantities.

Baneberry *(Actaea rubra)*. The berries may be red or white.

Biscuitroot
Lomatium species

Parsley Family
Umbelliferae

Excepting a few characteristics, biscuitroot is a typical member of the Parsley family. The flowers are borne in umbrella-shaped terminal inflorescences, ranging from white to yellow to pink or purple. The stems are hollow, and the pinnately divided, compound leaves commonly appear parsleylike (depending on species). More than seventy species of biscuitroot inhabit the West. Species frequently hybridize, making specific identification difficult and sometimes frightening, as several species of this plant share a striking resemblance to the highly poisonous hemlock parsley *(Conium maculatum)*. Unlike hemlock parsley and most other umbelliferaes, biscuitroots usually grow in dry, rocky, often steep habitats. Hemlock parsley and other toxic umbels generally require consistently moist, deep soils, without which they cannot survive. This is not to say that biscuitroot cannot share house with its poisonous cousins, as biscuitroot too will grow in moist soils. After checking your local plant key for species in your area, a simple first-step rule applies to the identification of the *Lomatium* genus by habitat: if the soil is dry and void of most organic matter, it is probably a lomatium. If the plant is growing in moist soil, it very well could be a highly poisonous plant, so leave it alone. Once the habitat characteristics have been determined, identification can be substantiated further by distinctive physical characteristics, such as the large (½- to ¾-inch) oval seeds of many species, or the unique overall appearance of species such as *L. triternatum*, which has leaves that are two to three times divided into linear, almost hairlike segments. The largest member of the genus, *L. dissectum*, may grow to 40 inches tall and can readily be differentiated from smaller lomatiums (such as *L. cous*) by its size.

Blooms: May to July.

Habitat and Range: Generally found in dry, rocky soils. Many species are common to rockslides and steep hillsides, sometimes growing directly from fissures in vertical escarpments. From British Columbia through the Rockies to Arizona and west into the mountains of California.

Edibility: Once positive identification can be guaranteed, the roots of all varieties may be consumed, either raw or cooked. American Indians valued biscuitroot as an important staple. As the common name implies, they also dried and ground the root into a coarse, starchy flour, which was used in preparing a variety of dishes. Although all species are edible, most people will find some of them too resinous to enjoy. *Lomatium cous* is one of the most palatable, with fibrous roots that have a mildly sweet, ricelike flavor. The leaves and stems may also be eaten as a substitute for parsley.

Medicinal Uses: The large, thick taproots of *L. dissectum* have a long, revered history as a medicine. Blackfeet Indians called it Big Medicine, for its strong actions against respiratory infections. Today, herbalists regard it highly as a strong respiratory antimicrobial, expectorant, and antiviral medicine. Laboratory studies have shown it as active against a wide variety of bacteria. None of the other lomatiums are universally recognized as medicine.

WARNING! Many biscuitroot species share similar appearances with highly poisonous Parsley family relatives. Positive identification must be absolute before ingesting this plant in any form.

Big Medicine *Lomatium dissectum*

Lomatium triternatum

Bittersweet
Solanum dulcamara

Nightshade Family
Solanaceae

Bittersweet is a climbing perennial that may grow to 10 feet. Most commonly it grows in tangled thickets at the edges of irrigation ditches or along streambanks. The leaves are dark green, have short petioles, and are spade shaped, commonly with winglike lobes at their bases. The flowers look characteristically like those of garden variety potatoes or tomatoes (which are also in the Solanaceae family), with yellow anthers protruding in front of backward-pointing, purple petals. The bright red, ¼- to ½-inch berries tend to ripen only a few at a time, giving the plant a colorful mix of green and red ornaments.

Blooms: Spring to midsummer.

Habitat and Range: A Eurasian import that continues to spread; common to moist soils in much of North America. In the West, it is particularly common from northern California north, and east into Idaho and Montana.

Toxicity: Like many members of the Nightshade family, bittersweet can be toxic if consumed in excess.

Medicinal Uses: Used in the correct applications and dosages by experienced herbal practitioners, this plant may be useful in the treatment of skin disorders, gout, rheumatism, bronchitis, and whooping cough. Scientific study has confirmed that this plant possesses anticancer qualities.

> **WARNING!** The toxic alkaloids and phytosterols in bittersweet may be damaging to the liver if misused. The berries are toxic in any quantity. This plant demands caution and respect.

Black Henbane
Hyoscyamus niger

Nightshade Family
Solanaceae

Black henbane, a 1- to 5-foot-tall annual or biennial weed, earned its common name from its distinctive yellowish brown flowers, which have purplish veins on their petals and dark (almost black) centers. The coarsely toothed or triangular-lobed, alternate leaves are tightly distributed along a stout central stalk. The entire plant often has a pungent "dead" odor, which becomes stronger when the foliage is bruised. Fruits appear in early fall and look like 1-inch-long green pineapples.

Blooms: Flowers open in early spring, then commonly remain in bloom throughout the summer months.

Habitat and Range: First introduced from Europe, black henbane now inhabits pastures, roadsides, and various waste areas across the United States; sometimes cultivated for ornamental purposes, but more often considered a troublesome weed.

Toxicity: Very dangerous. Consumption in any quantity or form may have immediate sedative effects on the heart muscle, and may result in cardiac arrest.

Medicinal Uses: Although this plant is far too toxic for the layperson to pick and employ as an herbal medicine, black henbane has a long and important history as an official drug plant. Alkaloid constituents of this plant are isolated, extracted, and refined in pharmaceutical laboratories. Atropine, for example, is a drug in everyday use by mainstream doctors and paramedics to treat liver and kidney conditions, to dilate the pupils during eye examinations and surgeries, and, most important, to act as a cardiac antispasmodic in cases of life-threatening arrhythmias. Although advanced herbalists have used whole forms of this plant in very small quantities throughout the centuries, its use as an herbal medicine in any capacity remains limited to an experienced few.

> **WARNING!** Do not mess with this plant.

Bittersweet fruit *Solanum dulcamara*

Bittersweet *Solanum dulcamara*

Black Henbane *Hyoscyamus niger*

Castor Bean

Ricinus communis

Spurge Family
Euphoriaceae

This annual or perennial herb is characterized by large, palmately lobed leaves and spiny, reddish, ½- to 1-inch-long oval fruits, each containing three or fewer bean-shaped seeds. The flowers (and later, the fruits) are borne in densely clustered terminal racemes, with all of the female flowers clustered above the male flowers. In areas with long, warm growing seasons, castor beans are often found forming their own thickets, where individual plants may reach 12 feet tall.

Blooms: February to July, variable according to climate and precipitation.

Habitat and Range: An exotic import that has escaped cultivation throughout the southern half of the United States; particularly common in waste areas of the South and Southwest.

Toxicity: This plant is extremely toxic, the fruits in particular. One bean may be fatal to a child. Frequent cases of contact dermatitis have been recorded as a result of handling this plant.

Medicinal Uses: Castor bean is still commercially cultivated for its oil, which is pressed from the seeds by a process that separates the oil from most of the plant's toxic proteins. Many of us have unpleasant childhood memories of castor oil used as a laxative (or was it for punishment?). This practice is no longer popular, as modern studies have determined that the toxicity of the oil far outweighs its benefits. Topical applications of castor oil, however, remain popular with naturopathic physicians, herbalists, and folk healers, who use it in compresses called castor oil packs to treat various forms of blockage or excess in the body. For example, in the treatment of ovarian cysts, a castor oil pack is applied to the abdomen, covered with plastic, then left on the body for several minutes each day while the patient rests. This is believed to shrink the cysts, but exactly how it works is speculative. The external application of the oil is also said to be useful for hemorrhoids, abscesses, boils, and ringworm. Castor oil is commercially available as an over-the-counter remedy.

> **WARNING!** Avoid all contact with castor bean plant. Anyone who is suspected of having ingested the fruits or seeds should be rushed to a hospital immediately.

Castor Bean *Ricinus communis*

Castor Bean *Ricinus communis*

Clematis
Clematis columbiana

Buttercup Family
Ranunculaceae

Also known as virgin's bower, traveler's joy, or pepper vine, clematis is a climbing perennial with strong, vinelike woody stems typically seen entwined in the branches of neighboring trees and shrubs. Several species of clematis grow in North America, both native and introduced. Of the wild varieties, *Clematis columbiana* is one of the most widespread of the western woodland species. *Clematis ligusticifolia*, a dweller of riparian thickets, is by far the most common and widespread of the lowland species. *Clematis columbiana* is best recognized by its showy lavender flowers, which instead of petals present four tapered sepals that look like petals, in an arrangement reminiscent of a paper lantern. After blooming, the flowers develop into silvery white seed-bearing plumes. The opposite leaves are on long petioles (leaf stems) and are divided into three pointed leaflets, each with one side indented and a rounded base. The climbing stems may reach 8 feet long. *Clematis ligusticifolia* produces much smaller, less conspicuous cream-colored flowers, although the overall plant is much larger (stems up to 20 feet).

Blooms: May to July.

Habitat and Range: *Clematis columbiana* grows on wooded hillsides, particularly in coniferous forests of the Northwest at subalpine elevations, from British Columbia to Oregon, and east into Montana and Wyoming. *Clematis ligusticifolia* is widespread across the western half of North America, in streamside thickets and ravines from below sea level in the deserts of the Southwest, and to about 4,000 feet in mountain areas of New Mexico and north to British Columbia.

Toxicity: Although clematis earned the common name pepper vine because early travelers used it to spice up salads, the entire genus contains strong chemical constituents that can irritate skin and mucous membranes. Ingestion can cause internal bleeding.

Medicinal Uses: This plant is essentially toxic, but many advanced practitioners claim that properly formulated preparations may be useful in the treatment of migraine headaches. Although no longer used in mainstream medicine, the liniment was once used by physicians for treating nervous disorders and skin eruptions.

WARNING! Consumption of this plant may cause internal bleeding.

Clematis   *Clematis columbiana*

Columbine

Aquilegia species

Buttercup Family

Ranunculaceae

Columbines are one of the most easily recognized spring flowers. Ranging from white to crimson red or dark blue (depending on species), the nodding flowers appear inverted, with five sepals curving backward, five petals extending erectly outward, and yellow stamens hanging from the center of the flowers like dangling tassels. The seed-bearing fruits are presented as capsules. The leaves are distinctive, too, compounded in groups of two or three with each leaf three-lobed.

Blooms: April to June.

Habitat and Range: Unless it has been introduced, columbine is generally a forest plant. At least eight species are distributed in the West, in moist meadows and woodlands from Alaska to the mountains of Utah, Colorado, and California.

Toxicity: Although the flowers are safe when consumed in small quantities, the rest of the plant can be very toxic, particularly the seeds and roots.

Edibility: This plant demands caution, but the flowers are sweet and can be consumed in small quantities—they make a beautiful garnish on salads.

Medicinal Uses: Ancient European history indicates that columbine plants were used to treat a wide array of ailments, from heart palpitations to boils and ulcers. Columbine is seldom used in modern herbalism, probably because of the risk of toxicity.

WARNING! Therapeutic use of columbine is best left in the history books and definitely should not be attempted by the layperson.

Red Columbine *Aquilegia formosa*

Death Camas
Zigadenus species

Lily Family
Liliaceae

Death camas is a 6- to 24-inch-tall perennial that arises from dark brown bulbs in early spring. The plants first emerge as two angular, grasslike blades, later developing a central stalk that will bear several smaller grasslike leaves and an elongated terminal cluster of bell-shaped *(Zigadenus venenosus)* or wheel-shaped *(Z. elegans)* cream-colored flowers. Early in its growth (as the "camas" in its common name implies), death camas looks similar to the edible blue camas *(Camassia quamash)*, except that it is much smaller and can thrive in much drier habitats. Once in bloom, the differences between the two species are obvious. The similarities between death camas and members of the *Allium* genus (wild onion) are far more frightening, as both plants share the same habitat, often growing side-by-side and appearing similar at first glance when young. Both plants exhibit grasslike leaves, but on close inspection, you can see that the leaves of death camas are more erect and distinctively angled at their midribs, whereas wild onion's are flattened or hollow and generally cannot support their own weight. The flowers of the two are distinctly different, too, with wild onion's either nodding or arranged in a globelike inflorescence. Appearance aside, wild onions are easy to distinguish from death camas by their typical onion odor: if it does not smell distinctively like an onion, do not eat it.

Blooms: April to June.

Habitat and Range: Grasslands, shrub lands, and open forest clearings up to timberline. Two species of death camas are widespread from British Columbia to Mexico and east into Nebraska.

Toxicity: Very poisonous. This plant may be fatal if ingested.

Medicinal Uses: None. However, some Inidan tribes believe that the plant repels evil spirits when placed around the perimeter of camp.

WARNING! Do not mess with this plant.

Death Camas *Zigadenus venenosus*

Dogbane

Apocynum species

Dogbane Family

Apocynaceae

Dogbane is a spreading perennial with opposite leaves and umbel-shaped inflorescences of small greenish white to pink, tubular or bell-shaped flowers. Plants may reach 40 inches tall, but average less than 18 inches. Of the four species in the West, *Apocynum androsaemifolium* (creeping dogbane) is perhaps the most distinctive. The leaves of this species are up to 4 inches long, lance shaped or narrowly oblong, and spread or droop from their short petioles as if the entire plant has wilted. This makes for a unique appearance. When the leaves turn to bright yellow or red in late summer, dense stands of these plants can be spectacular.

Blooms: June to August.

Habitat and Range: Widespread across most of North America, with habitat varying from species to species. *Apocynum androsaemifolium* is predominantly a dryland, sun-loving variety of the mountain foothills. The most common and widespread variety, *A. canabinum* (common dogbane), prefers half-shaded, riparian habitats.

Toxicity: Dogbane contains cymarin, a substance that causes cardiac arrhythmia.

Medicinal Uses: Despite its toxicity, dogbane has been scientifically shown to possess antitumor properties. Advanced clinical herbalists sometimes use preparations of dogbane internally as a vasoconstrictor, diuretic, and cardiac stimulant (similar to digitalis), but this use by anyone except a qualified expert is strongly discouraged. Some people believe the topical application of the root tea will promote hair growth by mildly irritating the hair follicles and stimulating blood circulation in the scalp.

> **WARNING!** Dogbane is a cardiogenic toxin and should not be ingested as a food in any quantity. Although this plant shows promise in the laboratory and has been safely used by herbalists, it remains dangerous to all but the seasoned professional.

Creeping Dogbane *Apocynum androsaemifolium*

False Hellebore

Veratrum viride

Lily Family
Liliaceae

The coarse, strongly veined leaves of false hellebore clasp the unbranched, central stalk of the plant in a fashion similar to a corn stalk, a characteristic that has earned it the alternate common name corn lily. Basal leaves may grow to 12 inches long, with leaves of the upper plant progressively smaller toward the top of the plant. The entire plant may grow to 5 feet and is somewhat hairy in texture. The terminal flowers are very small, green to yellowish, and borne on side branches at the top of the plant. The fruits are ¾ to 1½ inches long and contain yellowish, winged seeds.

Blooms: June to August.

Habitat and Range: Prefers deep, moist mountain soils; common to wet mountain meadows, swamps, and streambanks, from Alaska south to the mountains of southern California *(Veratrum californicum)*, and east throughout the Rocky Mountains. Also in the eastern half of North America, from Quebec to North Carolina.

Toxicity: False hellebore is very toxic; its juice was sometimes used by Indians to poison arrows before combat. Alkaloids in this plant have cardiac sedative qualities that may prove fatal if ingested.

Medicinal Uses: Despite its extreme toxicity, this plant was historically used as an analgesic, anticonvulsive, and, in very dilute concentrations, as a sore throat remedy. Today, it is used in meticulously formulated pharmaceutical drugs to slow the heartbeat and lower blood pressure. The powdered root is used as an insecticide.

Look-Alike Plants: At early stages of growth, false hellebore shares a frightening resemblance with several other members of the Lily family, including false Solomon's seal, twisted-stalk, and glacier lily. Although it is possible to taxonomically "key out" the differences between this plant and edible look-alikes at any stage of growth, the differences are often too dangerously small to mention here. I am an advocate of hands-on familiarity, and until you can recognize the differences between various lilies—that intimate knowledge you gain through day-to-day and season-to-season recognition—my advice is to wait until plants in this family are fully mature before attempting identification for ingestion purposes.

WARNING! Do not mess with this plant.

Gromwell

Lithospermum species

Borage Family
Boraginaceae

Also known as puccoon, this plant is often inconspicuous among grasses and other flora throughout its growth. Once they are picked out from their neighbors, gromwells are easy to recognize by their tightly arranged, narrowly lance-shaped to linear alternate leaves, and unique flowers. The entire, 4- to 24-inch-tall plant is covered with fine hairs, which gives the foliage a gray green appearance. The flowers are ⅛ to ¼ inch wide, have five petals, and are borne in the uppermost leaf axils or in terminal clusters. Their color ranges from white to bright yellow, but most commonly is a drab, yellowish green.

Blooms: May to July.

Habitat and Range: Open forest clearings and grasslands, up to about 6,500 feet from British Columbia south into California and throughout the Rocky Mountain States.

Toxicity: Although this plant has a long history of use as a medicine, it contains potentially toxic alkaloids that may cause internal bleeding, and estrogen-like constituents that interfere with hormonal balances in the female reproductive system.

Medicinal Uses: Lakota and Cheyenne Indians used topical preparations of various species of *Lithospermum* to treat open wounds, burns, paralysis, and rheumatic ailments. Shoshone Indians used the tea to treat diarrhea and as a female contraceptive. Following scientific research, a European variety *(L. arvensis)* has been used as an oral contraceptive (in central Europe); its estrogenic actions are said to suppress the menstrual cycle.

> **WARNING!** Given its dramatic hormonal effects in the body, and the concentrated presence of toxic compounds, gromwell cannot be safely approached as a medicine in the absence of further scientific research.

False Hellebore   *Veratrum viride*

Wayside Gromwell   *Lithospermum ruderale*

Hemlock Parsley
Conium maculatum

Parsley Family
Umbelliferae

The highly poisonous hemlock parsley (also known as poison hemlock) is why many herbalists and wild food foragers avoid all umbelliferaes. It presents several characteristics that typify several edible members of its family. Like others in the parsley clan, hemlock parsley has umbrella-shaped or flat-topped, terminal clusters of small white flowers and hollow stems. The leaves are divided several times into small leaflets, giving them the typical appearance of parsley, carrottops, or ferns used in floral arrangements. The plants may grow more than 5 feet tall, and may or may not have purple splotches on their usually multibranched stems. The taproots may be carrotlike, but usually are not and instead are divided and stringy. Many field guides say the plant has a "dead animal–like odor," but this is not always the case, and odor should not be used as a definitive reference here.

Blooms: May to July.

Habitat and Range: Consistently moist soils, often in standing water. Common to irrigation ditches, roadsides, cultivated fields, meadows, marshes, and disturbed sites up to subalpine elevations across North America.

Toxicity: Highly poisonous. May cause vomiting, convulsions, difficulty in breathing, coma, or death if ingested in *any* quantity.

Medicinal Uses: None.

Look-Alike Plants: Hemlock parsley resembles its edible and medicinal cousins, osha (*Ligusticum* species), and biscuitroot (*Lomatium* species). Unlike osha, however, the roots of hemlock parsley do not present us with the telltale hairlike, dead leaf matter that osha has surrounding its root crowns (see osha). And unlike biscuitroot, hemlock parsley requires a more consistent moisture supply and has small, ⅛-inch, ribbed seeds (see biscuitroot). Hemlock parsley also shares a frightening resemblance to several other umbels. A rule of survival: If it looks carrotlike or fernlike, beware. Ask for hands-on assistance from a plant expert before ingesting anything that resembles this plant.

> **WARNING!** Hemlock parsley is extremely toxic in any quantity and may be fatal if ingested. Wash your hands thoroughly afterward if you handle this plant.

Hemlock Parsley *Conium maculatum*

Jimsonweed
Datura meteloides

Nightshade Family
Solanaceae

Jimsonweed is a coarse annual with distinctive toothed or lobed, 4- to 8-inch, oblong, grayish green alternate leaves. Its 1- to 5-inch-long, trumpet-shaped, pink or white axillary flowers resemble those of domestic morning glory (*Ipomoea* species). The spiny, 1- to 2-inch-long, egg-shaped fruits contain long, flat seeds.

Blooms: May to September.

Habitat and Range: Abandoned fields and waste areas across North America.

Toxicity: This plant has strong narcotic properties, and ingesting it may lead to convulsions, hallucinations, respiratory arrest, or death. It has earned recognition in recent years among drug users, who have named the plant "hell's bells." It is unfortunately becoming increasingly popular among teenagers who are seeking hallucinogenic experiences. In many cases, experimentation results in tragedy, and most who survive the experience have learned how the plant earned its less than attractive street name. The effects produced by this plant are anything but recreational. I have seen the results while working in emergency services. This stuff is dangerous and does not provide a "trip" to anyplace nice (they don't pump stomachs in nirvana, do they?). Don't mess with it.

Medicinal Uses: Despite being potentially deadly, jimsonweed has important medicinal values. The plant contains hyoscyamine, atropine, and several other alkaloids used in scientifically refined antispasmodic drugs (see also black henbane). It also contains scopolamine, an antivertigo compound commonly used to treat motion sickness and other conditions involving equilibrium.

WARNING! Do not mess with this plant.

Jimsonweed   *Datura meteloides*

Osha
Ligusticum canbyi

Parsley Family
Umbelliferae

Osha (pronounced oh-SHAW) exhibits characteristics typical of the Parsley family: umbrella-shaped inflorescences of tiny white flowers atop hollow, 1- to 3-foot stems that bear fernlike, pinnately compound leaves. The basal leaves are up to 8 inches long and are finely divided two or three times into deeply lobed leaflets. The leaves of the upper stem are smaller, with fewer divisions. Eight or more species of *Ligusticum* inhabit North America. Some are smaller than others, and some have leaves more finely divided and carrotlike *(L. tenuifolium)*, but they all share habitat and an uncomfortably similar appearance with their cousin, hemlock parsley, or poison hemlock *(Conium maculatum)*. Differentiating osha from this deadly look-alike strongly depends on personal familiarity and practical experience. Two characteristics, when combined, can be used to begin the identification process. Unlike any other members of the umbel clan, osha has dead leaf material surrounding the crown of its well-defined taproot, and a spicy, celery-like odor that closely resembles that of its cultivated relative, lovage *(Levisticum officinale)*.

Blooms: May to August, depending on climate and elevation.

Habitat and Range: Strictly a mountain plant that inhabits consistently moist, deep soils, osha requires at least partial shade and most frequently inhabits the upper limits of the subalpine zone (7,000 to 10,000 feet), especially toward the southern end of its range. From British Columbia south to the mountains of Oregon and Washington, and throughout the Rocky Mountains to the high mountains of New Mexico *(L. porteri)*. From Wyoming and Montana north, osha may be encountered as low as 5,000 feet.

Toxicity: Although not considered toxic, osha is commonly confused with plants that may prove fatal if ingested.

Edibility: The entire plant tastes like it smells—like strong, spicy celery. It may be used to flavor various dishes, but tends to be overpowering by itself.

Medicinal Uses: "Osha" is a Native American word meaning bear. Blackfeet and Salish Indians referred to this plant as "bear medicine," a term that was likely derived from their observations of bears eating it, presumably for medicinal purposes. The plant, like the bear, was prized as one of their most valuable and sacred sources of healing. It was used to treat various (and often serious) respiratory disorders, stomachache, fevers, and heartburn. Today, herbalists recognize it as a strong respiratory antiviral medicine, specifically useful against viral infections that are characterized by a deep, raspy, unproductive cough. This plant has been sensationalized beyond its true usefulness, and as a result, populations of osha are diminishing under market pressures.

> **WARNING! Osha can be very difficult to distinguish from extremely poisonous members of the Parsley family. Familiarity and hands-on experience are a necessity here. Do not ingest this plant unless you are absolutely confident you have the right plant.**

The flowers of osha *(Ligusticum canbyi)* are typical of the Parsley family.

The root crown of osha *(Ligusticum canbyi)* is surrounded with hairlike, dead leaf material.

Osha leaves *(Ligusticum canbyi)*

Pasqueflower
Anenome nuttalliana

Buttercup Family
Ranunculaceae

A unique and showy plant, pasqueflower often stands out in spectacular contrast to the low grasses of early spring. The solitary flower is light lavender on the inside surfaces of the petals and darker purple on the outside, with a bright yellow center (stamen). The flower is 2 to 3 inches in diameter and opens only when the sun is shining. The blossom appears proportionately large for the plant. The stem leaves also are unique, each with three deep divisions that are subdivided into several smaller divisions. The entire plant may reach only 10 inches high and is covered with silky white hairs.

Blooms: April to June.
Habitat and Range: Dry montane meadows, rarely above 5,000 feet.
Toxicity: Potentially very toxic. This plant is known to slow the heart when ingested.
Medicinal Uses: Although this plant is potentially toxic, it is also potentially useful as a medicine. I do not recommend its use, but pasqueflower's long history as a medicinal herb warrants attention beyond the scope of its physical beauty. As we learn to appreciate the attributes of such plants at levels beyond the superficial, we gain valuable insight into deeper values that translate to the well-being of the environment.

Pasqueflower was used by Blackfeet Indians to speed childbirth or induce abortion, which should immediately trigger a warning for anyone who might plan to use this plant. Pasqueflower was listed in the United States pharmacopoeia from 1882 to 1905 as a treatment for cataract, paralysis, rheumatism, syphilis, and several other ailments. It was used by Ponca and Omaha Indians in a broad spectrum of applications, particularly in the external treatment of sores and wounds, including those of the eyes. In modern phytotherapy, pasqueflower is sometimes used in small doses by the advanced practitioner as an antidepressant and sedative.

WARNING! Pasqueflower is known to slow the heart when ingested. Like all medicinal plants, it should never be used in the absence of proper training and qualified professional advice.

Pasqueflower   *Anenome nuttalliana*

Sagebrush
Artemisia tridentata

Sunflower Family
Compositae

Sagebrush is the classic range plant you frequently see in cowboy westerns. The West simply would not be the West without *Artemisia tridentata*. Let it be known once and for all that sagebrush and sage are two entirely different plants. Several species of *Artemisia* are referred to as sagebrush, sagewort, sageweed, and so on, because they smell similar to various *Salvia* species (sages), a genus of the unrelated Mint family (Labiatae).

The *Artemisia* genus is large and diverse but is generally divided into four categories: (1) true shrubs *(A. tridentata)*, (2) smaller, multistemmed herbs that produce sterile shoots from creeping rhizomes (*A. ludoviciana*, white sagewort; *A. vulgaris*, wormwood), (3) compact plants that grow in ground-hugging mats (*A. abisinthum*, sageweed), and (4) odorless, taprooted biennials or perennials (*A. campestris*, prairie sagewort). The strongly aromatic sagebrush *(A. tridentata)* is the largest (up to 4 feet) and most common shrub species of the West. Like other *Artemisia* species, it is distinguished by its silvery gray appearance and alternate leaves. The leaves of this species are uniquely divided into three parts at their tips, making positive identification easy. The tubular, yellowish flowers are small and borne in loosely arranged terminate inflorescences that tend to rise at equal lengths above the rest of the plant, often giving the shrub a flat-topped appearance when viewed from a distance.

Blooms: July to September.

Habitat and Range: In high deserts and dry mountain basins from British Columbia to Baja and east throughout the Rockies and the Dakotas. Commonly the predominant groundcover, stretching as far as the eye can see.

Toxicity: This plant is highly allergenic and, in rare cases, may cause dermatitis when applied to the skin. Taken internally, it can be toxic and may cause damage to the liver and digestive tract.

Medicinal Uses: Although generally regarded as toxic, most *Artemisia* species have been used at some time or other as medicine. Perhaps the most profound attribute sagebrush offers is its strong bacteriostatic quality. Used with caution as a skin wash or in other topical applications, *Artemisia* is believed to combat various forms of infection. American Indians used several varieties of this plant as a ceremonial smudge, to physically and spiritually cleanse the body of impurities and evil spirits. Taken internally, the leaf tea has been used to stop internal bleeding and rid the digestive system of parasites, but these practices are strongly discouraged by most modern-day herbalists.

Look-Alike Plants: Although the appearance of sagebrush is distinctive, its odor leads many people to believe it is a sage. Remember this: sagebrush and other *Artemisia* species have alternate leaves, but true sages (*Salvia* species) always have opposite leaves.

WARNING! Sagebrush taken internally can be toxic, and its use should be strictly limited to the experienced practitioner.

Big Sagebrush *Artemisia tridentata*

The unique, three-clefted leaves of *Artemisia tridentata*

Stinging Nettle
Urtica species

Nettle Family
Urticaceae

To the wild food forager who has learned to respect its sting and recognize its attributes, stinging nettle is a true delight. But to the unknowing explorer who haphazardly wanders into a stand of these plants, stinging nettle offers a crash course in plant identification (and contact dermatitis). The underside of the leaves and the stems of the plant are covered with thousands of tiny, hollow needlelike hairs that contain a combination of antigenic proteins and formic acid (the latter being the chosen weaponry of red ants). When contacted with sufficient force, these mini-hypodermics inject their contents, causing a sudden, burning rash on the skin. The pain and tiny blisters usually subside within an hour. For anyone who does not wish to take the crash course, here is a more subtle introduction to this species.

Stinging nettle is an erect plant that may grow as tall as 7 feet where conditions permit. It reproduces largely from its shallow rhizomes and commonly dense colonial patches. The opposite leaves are broadly lance shaped, with coarsely toothed margins. The flowers are borne at the leaf axils and appear as inconspicuous, brownish, drooping clusters. The stems are covered with fine, stinging hairs. Young plants often emerge reddish, turning green as they mature.

Blooms: Early to midspring.

Habitat and Range: Several species of *Urtica* grow in consistently moist, rich soils, often in roadside ditches or riparian habitats across most of North America. In the West, *U. dioica* is the predominant species.

Edibility: Despite its nasty sting, nettle is one of the most delicious and nutritious foods in nature's pantry. Cooking or thorough drying neutralizes the toxic constituents, and the entire plant may be prepared like spinach or in a pleasant tea. Stinging nettle is high in iron, calcium, potassium, manganese, and vitamins A, C, and D. Young plants are the most palatable, as the plants become tough and fibrous with age. This plant should not be consumed during or after its bloom stage, as the foliage then develops gritty particles (called "cystoliths") that may cause irritation to the urinary tract if ingested in large quantities.

Medicinal Uses: Herbalists regard this plant as an excellent nutritive tonic. The tea has a folkloric reputation as a menstrual flow regulator and postpartum tonic; the latter use can be justified in part by the trace minerals it replaces following childbirth. Indians sometimes whipped themselves with the fresh leaves and stems to counteract the pain and swelling of arthritis, the theory being that the pain-causing constituents were absorbed through the skin to activate a therapeutic effect. If nothing else, it probably took the arthritis sufferer's mind off his or her chronic ailment for a while.

WARNING! *Urtica* **species causes an immediate contact dermatitis if handled without gloves and proper clothing. The leaves and stems must be thoroughly dried or cooked before ingestion.**

Stinging Nettle   *Urtica dioica*

Young stinging nettle often has a reddish tint, and is
delicious and nutritious as a cooked green.

Tansy
Tanacetum vulgare

Sunflower Family
Compositae

Common tansy is a conspicuous, stout perennial quickly recognized by its flat-topped terminal clusters of bright yellow, ¼- to ½-inch-wide buttonlike flowers and its alternate, deeply divided and numerously segmented leaves. Look for the 1- to 6-foot-tall plants in dense stands in the waste areas where they commonly grow. The entire plant is strongly aromatic (much like mothballs or yarrow), especially when bruised.

Blooms: May to September.

Habitat and Range: Along roadsides and irrigation ditches, in pastures, and in any variety of moist waste areas across most of the United States and Canada. Introduced from Europe as an ornamental and medicinal market plant.

Toxicity: This plant contains oils that may cause contact dermatitis and can be damaging to the liver and digestive tract if taken internally in large enough quantities.

Medicinal Uses: Despite its potential toxicity, tansy has been used as a medicine for centuries. Its traditional uses include the treatment of weak kidneys, jaundice, and sore throat, but it is best known for its ability to rid the digestive tract of worms. Most contemporary herbalists have abandoned this plant in recognition that its toxicity outweighs its usefulness. The leaves are known to have insecticidal properties and may be decocted for use in the garden.

WARNING! Anything in the plant kingdom that can kill intestinal parasites can certainly cause harm to humans. Because of the toxicity of this plant, the FDA prohibits the sale of tansy as a food or medicine.

Common Tansy   *Tanacetum vulgare*

Water Hemlock

Cicuta douglasii

Parsley Family
Umbelliferae

Water hemlock is by far the most poisonous plant in North America. This is the stuff that killed Socrates. Surprisingly, few accidental accounts of water hemlock poisoning have been recorded in current history. Perhaps this is because of the collective fear this plant has instilled in many would-be herbalists and foragers, who in recognition of its frightening resemblance to angelica, osha, and sweetroot have elected to abandon the entire Parsley family. Water hemlock disguises itself well as any number of these useful cousins (particularly angelica), with its white, umbrella-shaped flower clusters, hollow 12- to 60-inch stems, and leaves that are pinnately divided two to three times into lance-shaped, sharply toothed leaflets. Although the differences between water hemlock and other edible or medicinal parsleys may seem to be minute, they are actually distinctive and easy to recognize. Water hemlock can be differentiated from all other members of the Umbelliferae family by its leaf veins, which meet or terminate *within the indentation between the teeth* of the leaf margins. Angelica and other umbels have leaf veins that terminate at the *outer tip of each tooth*. Angelica also has unique seeds (see angelica). Many field guides attempt to differentiate water hemlock from other umbels by using hollow, chambered roots and purple stem splotches as references. Forget it. My colleagues and I have seen many specimens of water hemlock that presented neither of these characteristics. Those references are inaccurate and potentially dangerous. Robyn Klein, a renowned American herbalist, taught me a catchy reminder of water hemlock's unique leaf veins: "Leaf vein to the tip, all is hip. Leaf vein to the cut, pain in the gut." It works for me.

Blooms: April to July.

Habitat and Range: Moist or wet soils; often in standing water and particularly common in irrigation ditches, along road margins, and in waste areas throughout most of North America.

Toxicity: As little as one-quarter teaspoon of the root may cause death in an adult human within fifteen minutes.

Medicinal Uses: None

WARNING! Water hemlock is extremely toxic in any quantity and may be fatal if ingested.

Water Hemlock   *Cicuta douglasii*

Water hemlock's unique leaf veins meet or terminate
within the marginal notches at the edge of the leaf.

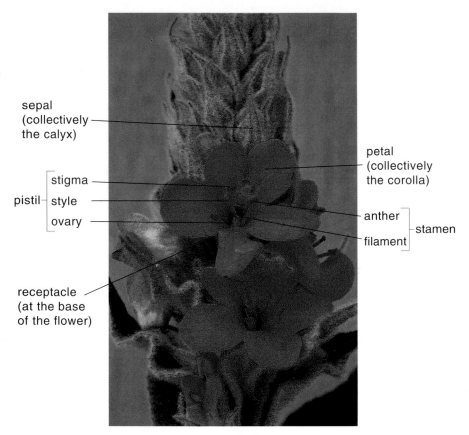

sepal
(collectively
the calyx)

petal
(collectively
the corolla)

stigma

pistil style

ovary

anther

filament

stamen

receptacle
(at the base
of the flower)

Anatomy of a flower

Glossary

action. See *medicinal action*

allopathy. The use of drugs or other means to antidote a disease or symptom, in a manner not necessarily cooperative with the body's natural functions. Antonym: homeopathy.

alluvial. The type of process where sedimentary materials, such as soil and rocks, are deposited or accumulated by flowing water.

alterative. An action that gradually alters an existing condition in the body. A "blood alterative" is often referred to as a "blood cleanser," as it alters the entrance of toxins and waste materials into the bloodstream, in most cases through stimulation of liver function.

alternate. In reference to leaves, alternate leaves are arranged along a stem at various distances from each another, but never opposite each other across the stem. (See salal and huckleberry photos.)

analgesic. A pain-relieving substance.

anesthetic. A substance that reduces painful sensitivity. Unlike general analgesics, anesthetics often can be applied locally. An injection of novocaine at the dentist is a local anesthetic.

annual. A plant that blooms, distributes its seeds, and then dies during its first and only year. Annuals depend solely on seed reproduction.

anther. The pollen-bearing organ at the end of the stamen, responsible for the distribution of pollen. The anther is usually yellow or orange and is the part bees seek out. (See evening primrose photo.)

anthropocentric. Regarding the human being as the central fact or final aim of the universe.

anticatarrhal. A substance capable of assisting the body in eliminating excess mucus from the upper respiratory tract, through anti-inflammatory actions on the mucous membranes that are responsible for the secretions.

antifungal. Capable of preventing or inhibiting fungal infections.

antihidrotic. Capable of preventing or inhibiting perspiration.

antihistamine. An herb or drug that alters histamine responses in the body, with the effect of reducing the discomforts of allergic reactions and, in some cases, motion sickness.

antimicrobial. An action that helps the body to resist, inhibit, or destroy pathogenic microbes. In holistic medicine, this term generally describes actions that assist the body in fighting bacteria, fungi, or viruses at their original point of infection.

antioxidant. A general, perhaps worn-out term referring to the ability of a substance to control or eliminate free radicals or reduce cellular oxidation in the body.

antipyretic. Capable of reducing fever.

antirheumatic. Capable of relieving the symptoms of rheumatic conditions, such as rheumatoid arthritis.

antiscorbutic. A substance that helps to prevent or cure scurvy or other imbalances relative to vitamin C deficiency.

antiseptic. Generally refers to substances that kill or inhibit the growth of pathogenic microbes. In holistic medicine, this term describes substances that interfere with bacterial infections regardless of the body's natural abilities to do so. In this context, antiseptic herbs are applied as allopathic remedies.

antispasmodic. Capable of relieving spasms.

antitussive. Capable of suppressing coughing.

antiviral. Capable of inhibiting the reproduction or activity of a virus.

astringent. Capable of tightening soft tissues of the body. Astringents are used to stop bleeding, to reduce inflammation, and to stop diarrhea.

axil. In plants, axil usually refers to the junction where a petiole or peduncle joins the stem. Many members of the Mint family, for example, present their flowers at the leaf axils (see field mint photo). These are referred to as axillary flowers. The flowers of licorice (*Glycyrrhiza* spp.) are presented on peduncles (pedicels), which are also borne from the leaf axils (see licorice photo).

bacteriostatic. Specifically acting to inhibit the multiplication of bacteria.

basal. Refers to the base of something. Basal leaves are the ones at the extreme lower end of a plant. They are usually the first true leaves to appear after germination.

biennial. A plant that blooms only during its second year of growth, and then dies.

bitter tonic. A substance that stimulates digestive functions, first in the mouth and later in the stomach and liver. Bitter tonics are traditionally used to aid digestion.

bracts. Modified or reduced leaflets usually associated with the flower of a plant, often located beneath the petals. (See thistle photo for a conspicuously bracted inflorescence.)

candida. A yeastlike genus of fungi that inhabit the vagina or digestive tract, or both, which under certain conditions may cause candidiasis, an acute or chronic yeast infection.

carcinogen, carcinogenic. A substance or agent that promotes the formation or growth of cancer.

cardiac tonic. Capable of strengthening the heart muscle or stimulating heartbeat, or both, in a manner beneficial to body functions.

carminative. A substance that aids in the expulsion of gas from the digestive tract, having a "carminative action" in the body.

catarrh. The excessive secretion of thick phlegm or mucus from inflamed mucous membranes. See *anticatarrhal*

cathartic. A synonym for laxative. This term generally is used to describe a strong laxative.

catkin. An elongated, often fuzzy, conelike flower usually lacking any distinguishable petals or sepals. Catkins are characteristic of the poplar and willow plant families. (See willow photo.)

chlorophyll. Any of an assortment of green pigments found in plants. Chlorophyll enables plants to photosynthesize.

cholagogue. Refers to substances that stimulate bile production in the liver.

circumboreal. The portion of the earth that includes the northern one-third of the planet.

coagulant. A substance capable of promoting blood clotting, converting blood from a liquid to a semisolid state.

compound. In reference to leaves, a compound leaf is composed of multiple, smaller leaf segments, often pinnately arranged pairs of leaflets. (See angelica, elderberry, and yarrow photos.)

concentric. Having a common center; circular. (See angelica, biscuitroot, and osha photos for concentric flower clusters.)

conifers. Trees and shrubs that bear their flowers and fruits in the form of scaly, conelike structures, which includes all members of the fir, pine, and cypress families.

constituent. A single element or a compound ingredient that is part of a whole. A medicinal constituent in a plant is an element or compound that makes the plant medicinally useful.

corm. A swollen, nutlike structure on the root systems of various plants. (See yampa photo.)

corolla. The collective petals, or rays, of a flower.

counterirritant. An irritant that distracts attention away from another irritant. Usually applied externally. A deep-heating, mentholatum muscle ointment is a counterirritant to the discomfort of aching muscles.

deciduous. Plants that lose their leaves once a year, at the end of the growing season.

decoction. An herbal preparation made by simmering plant material in water until maximum extraction of active constituents is achieved. This process is usually used for roots, barks, and seeds that are not water soluble enough for use in simple infusions (teas).

demulcent. A substance that provides a protective coating and is soothing to irritated tissues in the body.

dermatitis. Inflammation of the skin.

detritis. Loose fragments on the forest floor that result from the disintegration of rocks and forest debris.

diaphoretic. Capable of stimulating perspiration.

digestive tonic. A substance that aids digestion.

diuresis. The process by which the body eliminates waste and excesses through kidney function and subsequent urination.

diuretic. A substance that stimulates diuresis.

duff. Thick mats of detritis on the forest floor.

earth regenerator. A plant or other organism that helps to repair damaged habitat or soil structure.

ecosystem. The interdependent interaction between an ecological community and its environment.

elliptical. A longer-than-wide, oval-like shape with opposite ends that are equal in diameter. Not egg-shaped, but like a flattened circle.

emetic. A substance that induces vomiting.

emmenagogue. A substance that promotes menstruation.

emollient. A substance that soothes, protects, and softens the skin. The external counterpart to a demulcent.

evergreen. Any of a wide variety of plants (not just conifers) that retain most or all of their foliage through the winter months.

expectorant. A substance that helps to expel mucus from the upper respiratory tract.

filament. In a flower, the anther-bearing stalk of a stamen.

flavonoid. A chemical compound found in various forms in several plants. Flavonoid constituents are responsible for a wide range of medicinal actions and are generally responsible for the pigmentation of various red, yellow, or purple fruits. Also known as a bioflavonoid.

fruit. The seed-bearing structure of a plant.

glabrous. Lacking hairs. A characteristic of certain plant stems and leaves.

hemispherical. A shape that represents an equally divided half of a sphere. (See meadowsweet photo for an example of a hemispherical flower cluster.)

hemostatic. Refers to the stoppage of bleeding. Most herbal hemostatic substances work by astringent actions.

hepatic. A general term referring to medicinal action upon the liver.

homeopathy. A modality of medicine based on the theory that diseases can be cured by administering very minute doses of drugs that in a healthy person would produce symptoms similar to those of the disease.

hypertension. High blood pressure.

hypotension. Low blood pressure.

hypotensive. Capable of reducing blood pressure.

immunostimulant. Capable of stimulating and strengthening the autoimmune functions in the body. In herbal medicine, this term specifically refers to the medicinal support of infection-fighting antibodies in the bloodstream and tonification of the lymph system.

inflorescence. A flower or cluster of flowers.

infusion. A preparation made by pouring boiling water over herbs and allowing it to steep; a tea.

lanceolate. Lance-shaped; widest at the base, with sides tapering to a point. (See photos of pipsissewa, which has narrowly lanceolate leaves, and arnica, which has broadly lanceolate leaves.)

laxative. A substance that increases the frequency of bowel evacuation, generally through softening of fecal matter.

linear. Long and narrow. Referring to leaf characteristics, a linear leaf is too narrow to be considered "narrowly lanceolate," but instead resembles a blade of grass. (See biscuitroot *[L. triternatum]*, death camas, and wild onion photos.)

lobed. Referring to leaf characteristics, a lobed leaf has margins (outer edges) that are deeply indented in two or more places, but not as deeply as a palmate leaf.

Maple leaves are deeply lobed. (See alumroot, cow parsnip, and thimbleberry [p. 123] photos.)

lymph system. The system of the body responsible for the cleansing of tissues at the surface to cellular level and the production of various antibodies and white blood cells.

lymphatic. Refers to the lymph system. A lymphatic tonic strengthens the function of the lymph system.

medicinal action. Any of a variety of terms used to describe the effect an herb or other substance has on or in the body that may be considered therapeutic.

microbe. A microscopic organism, including various bacterias, viruses, fungi, and protozoans (such as *Giardia*).

microcosm. A tiny, often microscopic segment of an ecosystem represented by a specialized community of organisms; for example, the interrelated community of organisms in a patch of moss on a sheer rock cliff.

microecosystem. A small segment of an ecosystem. The relationship between the microorganisms on a dead tree and their environment is an example of a microecosystem.

mucilaginous. Containing mucilage, a sticky-oily substance often used in herbal medicine to soothe and protect irritated tissues. Mucilaginous herbs are generally used as emollients or demulcents.

nephritic. Of or relating to the kidneys.

nervine. Refers to substances that are tonic to the nervous system.

noxious weed. A term used in reference to generally hateful plant species we do not like and want to eradicate.

ointment. Somewhere between a liquid extract and a salve. An ointment is a thickened herbal extract that is too loose to hold its form without a container.

open-pollinated. Plant species that have not been genetically altered (nonhybridized) and are capable of reproducing in true form from generation to generation.

opposite. Referring to leaf characteristics, opposite leaves are arranged directly across from each other at regular intervals along the stem of the plant. (See arnica, field mint, and heal-all photos.)

ovate. Oval-shaped. (See hawthorn and serviceberry photos.)

palmate. A shape that resembles the human hand with fingers extended. A palmate leaf has margins deeply indented nearly to its base. (See coltsfoot and motherwort photos.)

pathogenic microbes. Microscopic organisms that act negatively on or in the body; harmful, infectious bacterias, fungi, and viruses are all pathogenic microbes.

peduncle. The stemlike structure that holds the fruit or flowers of many plants. Also commonly known as a pedicel. (See catnip and twisted-stalk photos.)

perennial. A plant that returns from its rootstock year after year. Perennials reproduce by seed and root reproduction.

petals. The bractlike inner segments of a flower; usually the most colorful part.

petiole. The part of a plant generally viewed as a leaf stem; it joins the leaf to the stem or root crown of the plant. (See photos of arrowleaf balsamroot and oxeye daisy, which have proportionally long petioles, and skullcap and heal-all, which have short or nearly absent petioles.)

pH. A numerical measurement of acidity or alkalinity. Relating to soil, a pH level of 7.0 is regarded as neutral.

photosynthesis. The process by which plants convert solar energy to carbohydrates.

pinnate. A compound leaf pattern where leaflets are arranged in opposing pairs along two sides of an axis. (See angelica, elderberry, valerian, and watercress photos.)

pollinator-attractor. A plant that is particularly attractive to insects and other organisms vital to pollination between plants.

poultice. An herbal preparation made by mashing plant materials with a liquid (usually water) to form a wet paste.

purgative. An extremely, perhaps violently, strong laxative with uncontrollable effect. Purgatives generally cause abdominal cramping and near-incontinent conditions. They are usually reserved by herbalists for use only in dire circumstances.

raceme. A flower cluster in which individual flowers have stalks and are attached to an elongated axis or stem. (See false Solomon's seal photo.)

ray. The extended, bladelike petal of a ray flower. (See photos of arnica and arrowleaf balsamroot, both with yellow rays, and oxeye daisy, with white rays.)

refrigerant. Capable of cooling the body temperature, usually by means of perspiration.

rhizome. An underground stem that extends itself horizontally. Crabgrass is an excellent example of a rhizomatous plant.

riparian habitat. An ecosystem in proximity to a consistent source of water (such as floodplains, streambanks, lakeshores, and marshes).

rosette. Referring to leaves, those which emerge in an overlay pattern resembling the shape of a rose flower. (See mullein and oxeye daisy photos.)

rubifacient. A substance that reddens and heats the skin when applied topically. A mustard pack is a classic example of a rubifacient.

salve. A preparation consisting of an herbal extract (usually an infusion or decoction) that has been thickened to the consistency of butter.

saponin. A glycoside plant compound. Present in many species of plants, saponins are characterized by their soaplike nature. Although many types of saponin have medicinally useful properties, many may also be irritating to the digestive tract and may cause toxic reactions if ingested.

sedative. An action that calms the nerves to help a person relax.

sepal. A modified leaf (usually green) that encloses a flower bud. Some plants have sepals that are more conspicuous than their flowers; for example, coptis (with green sepals) and bunchberry (with white sepals).

simple. Referring to leaf characteristics, a simple leaf has margins (outer edges) that are void of any serrations, divisions, or lobes. Take it literally: a simple leaf is a basic leaf.

sitz bath. A method of bathing where only the pelvic area of the body is immersed. Astringent herbs are sometimes used in sitzbath therapies for treatment of hemorrhoids, postpartum swelling, and other types of inflammation below the waist.

stamen. The male, pollen-bearing part of a flower, which collectively consists of an anther and a filament.

stigma. The female, pollen-receptive part of a flower, which is usually at the upper-most part of the flower center.

stimulant. A general term used to describe the increase of functional activity.

stratification. A germination process by which a seed must be subjected to a prolonged period of cold (often freezing) temperatures and moisture to break its dormancy.

Streptococcus. A genus of gram-positive, spherically shaped bacteria in microscopic chains. Most forms of *Streptococcus* are normally present and harmless in the body, while others, such as *S. pneumoniae* (bacterial pneumonia), are potentially deadly.

styptic. An agent that causes bleeding to stop by making tissues contract rapidly; essentially the same as an astringent.

subalpine. A general term for the ecological zone that lies below timberline in montaine areas. Exactly where the subalpine zone begins and ends is often un-clear and arguable among botanists, who generally differentiate subalpine from alpine zones by marker species, elevation, and climatic variances. The subalpine zone ends where dense stands of conifers become sparse or nonexistent at higher elevations.

symbiosis. A relationship in which two dissimilar organisms live together for mutual benefit.

terminate. Referring to flowers that are the absolute end-tips of plant stems. Also referred to as terminal. (See angelica, arrowleaf balsamroot, bee balm, and heal-all photos.)

tincture. An herbal preparation made by soaking plant material in a liquid solvent (called a menstruum) to extract active medicinal constituents. Commonly referred to as herbal extracts, tinctures may be made from menstruums of alcohol, glycerin, or vinegar. The type of menstruum used for a particular herb depends on the chemical or physical structure of the herb, or both. Alcohol-based menstruums usually yield the strongest herb tinctures and have the longest shelf life.

tonic. A general term for a nourishing substance that invigorates and increases the tone and strength of tissues and improves the function of one or more body systems.

umbel. Referring to flowers, umbel means umbrella-shaped. True umbels consist of tiny florets, each extending an equal distance from a common point to form dense clusters (see angelica, cow parsnip, and osha photos). I have used the terms umbel and umbel-like loosely, to include flowers that appear umbrella shaped regardless of the "true" criteria.

uterine stimulant. Capable of stimulating contraction of the uterus.

uterotonic. Tonic to the uterus.

vasoconstrictor. Capable of tightening the walls of blood vessels. Opposite of vasodilator.

vasodilator. Capable of dilating or widening blood vessels. Opposite of vasoconstrictor.

vulnerary. Refers to various actions that promote the healing of wounds.

Bibliography and Recommended Reading

Belzer, Thomas J. *Roadside Plants of Southern California*. Missoula: Mountain Press, 1984.

Buchman, Dian Dincin. *Herbal Medicine*. New York: Gramercy Publishing, 1980.

Castleman, Michael. *The Healing Herbs*. Emmaus, Pa.: Rodale Press, 1991.

Dawson, Ronald L. *Nature Bound: Pocket Field Guide*. Boise, Idaho: OMNIgraphics, 1985.

Densmore, Frances. *How Indians Use Wild Plants for Food, Medicine, and Crafts*. New York: Dover, 1974.

Dorn, Robert D. *Vascular Plants of Montana*. Cheyenne, Wyo.: Mountain West Publishing, 1984.

Duke, James A., and Steven Foster. *Eastern/Central Medicinal Plants*. Peterson Field Guide Series. Boston: Houghton Mifflin, 1990.

Foster, Steven. *Herbal Renaissance*. Layton, Utah: Gibbs Smith, 1993.

Gladstar, Rosemary. *Herbal Healing for Women*. New York: Simon & Schuster, 1993.

Green, James. *The Male Herbal*. Freedom, Calif.: The Crossing Press, 1991.

Grieve, Mrs. M. *A Modern Herbal*. Vols. 1 and 2. New York: Dover, 1971.

Harrington, H. D. *Edible Native Plants of the Rocky Mountains*. Albuquerque: University of New Mexico Press, 1967.

Hart, Jeff. *Montana: Native Plants and Early Peoples*. Helena: Montana Historical Society, 1976.

Hitchcock, Leo C., and Arthur Cronquist. *Flora of the Pacific Northwest*. Seattle: University of Washington Press, 1973.

Hoffmann, David. *An Elder's Herbal*. Rochester, Vt.: Healing Arts Press, 1993.

———. *The New Holistic Herbal*. Rockport, Mass.: Element Books, 1990.

Kindscher, Kelly. *Medicinal Wild Plants of the Prairie*. Lawrence: University Press of Kansas, 1992.

Little, Elbert L. *The Audubon Society Guide to North American Trees, Western Region*. New York: Knopf, 1988.

Lust, John. *The Herb Book*. 20th ed. New York: Bantam, 1987.

Mabey, Richard. *The New Age Herbalist*. New York: Collier Books, 1988.

Mills, Simon Y. *Out of the Earth.* New York: Viking, 1991.

Moore, Michael. *Medicinal Plants of the Desert and Canyon West.* Santa Fe: Museum of New Mexico Press, 1989.

———. *Medicinal Plants of the Mountain West.* 6th ed. Santa Fe: Museum of New Mexico Press, 1988.

———. *Medicinal Plants of the Pacific West.* Santa Fe, N.Mex.: Red Crane Books, 1993.

Mowrey, Daniel B. *Herbal Tonic Therapies.* New Canaan, Conn.: Keats Publishing, 1993.

Schofield, Janice J. *Discovering Wild Plants: Alaska, Canada, the Northwest.* Anchorage: Alaska Northwest Books, 1989.

Schultes, Richard Evans. *Medicines from the Earth.* Revised ed. New York: McGraw-Hill, 1983.

Spellenberg, Richard. *The Audubon Society Field Guide to North American Wildflowers.* New York: Knopf, 1979.

Strickler, Dee. *Forest Wildflowers.* Columbia Falls, Mont.: Flower Press, 1988.

Taylor, Ronald J. *Northwest Weeds.* Missoula: Mountain Press, 1990.

———. *Sagebrush Country.* Missoula: Mountain Press, 1992.

Taylor, Ronald J., and George W. Douglas. *Mountain Plants of the Pacific Northwest.* Missoula: Mountain Press, 1995.

Tilford, Gregory L. *The EcoHerbalist's Fieldbook: Wildcrafting in the Mountain West.* Conner, Mont.: Mountain Weed Publishing, 1993.

Whitson, Tom D. *Weeds of the West.* Rev. ed. Newark, Calif.: Western Society of Weed Science, 1992.

Willard, Terry. *Edible and Medicinal Plants of the Rocky Mountains and Neighbouring Territories.* Calgary, Alberta, Can.: Wild Rose, 1992.

Index

abrasions, 62
abscesses, 188
Achillea millefolium, 166–67
Actaea rubra, 142, 182–83
adder's tongue, 64
Adiantum capillus-veneris, 94
   jordanii, 94
   pedatum, 94–95
Agastache foeniculum, 102
   urticifolia, 102–3
AIDS, 4, 130
alcoholism, 46
alder, 12–13, 124
alkaloids, 32, 40, 126, 186, 198, 202;
   bitter, 104; carcinogenic, 8, 78, 144;
   in broccoli, 8; in spinach, 9
allergenic plants, 66
allergies, 9
Allium cernuum, 161
   species, 160, 194
Alnus rhombifolia, 12
   rubra, 12
   sinuata, 12–13
   tenuifolia, 12
alteratives, blood, 24, 124, 134, 152,
   168
Althea officinalis, 94
alumroot, 12–13
amaranth, 14–15
Amaranthus retroflexus, 14–15
Amelanchier alnifolia, 134–35
American ginseng, 50
American speedwell, 14–15
analgesics, 22, 26, 96, 100, 114, 116,
   124, 164, 166, 198
Anaphalis margaritacea, 108–9
Anenome nuttalliana, 206–7
anesthetic, 42
angelica, 214, 178–79

Angelica species, 178–79
angina pectoris, 70
Antennaria species, 108
Anthemis cotula, 110
antiallergenic, 90
antibacterial, 64, 90. *See also* antimicrobial
antibiotics, 3
anticancer agents, 22, 186
anticonvulsive, 90, 198
antidepressant, 206
antidote, 22
antigenic proteins, 210
antihistamines, 38, 106, 108
anti-inflammatory, 12, 22, 56, 60, 72,
   78, 90, 108, 112, 114, 118, 134, 172
antimicrobial, 40, 64, 102, 104, 128,
   148; respiratory, 184
antioxidant, 44, 114
antiseptic, 16, 18, 62, 80, 97, 128, 160
antispasmodic, 62, 82, 90, 110, 136,
   178, 182, 202
antitumor agents, 3, 12, 44, 64, 70, 124,
   148, 152, 196
antitussive, 90
antivertigo compound, 202
antiviral, 52, 54, 130; respiratory, 184,
   204
anxiety, 136, 150
aphrodisiac, 92
Apocynaceae, 108, 196
Apocynum androsaemifolium, 196–97
appetite stimulant, 88
Aquilegia formosa, 192–93
Araliaceae, 50
Arctium minus, 24–25
Arctostaphylos manzanita, 86
   uva-ursi, 86–87, 132
Aristolochiaceae, 156

arnica, 180–81
Arnica cordifolia, 180–81
    latifolia, 180
arrowleaf balsamroot, 7, 16–17
Artemisia abisinthum, 208
    campestris, 208
    ludoviciana, 208
    tridentata, 128, 208–9
    vulgaris, 128, 208
arteriosclerosis, 70
arthritis, 38, 46, 56, 172, 210
artichoke, 144
Asarum caudatum, 156–57
Asclepiadaceae, 96
Asclepias fascicularis, 96
    speciosa, 96–97
    syriaca, 96
asparagus, 8
aspirin, 96, 114, 164
asthma, 38, 56, 62, 90, 97, 102, 108
astringent, 12, 19, 29, 43, 56, 60, 62,
    68, 70, 72, 80, 86, 102, 108, 110,
    120, 132, 134, 140, 154, 162, 163
atropine, 8, 186, 202

bachelor's buttons, 88
bacteriostatic, 44, 64, 162, 208. *See
    also* antimicrobial; antiseptic
balm of Gilead, 114
Balsamorrhiza sagittata, 16–17
bamboo shoots, 28
baneberry, 142, 182–83
Barberry family, 104
basketry, 16, 172
bath rinse, 82
bear berry, 86
beargrass, 16–17
bear medicine, 204
beaver tails, 118
bedstraw, northern, 36
bee balm, 18–19, 28
beets, 169
Berberidaceae, 104
Berberis aquifolium, 104–5
    nervosa, 104
    repens, 104–5
bergamot, wild, 18
beta-carotene, 62, 134
betony, 92

betulin, 12
Big Medicine, 184
biliary function, stimulation of, 168
bile production, 104
Birch family, 12
Birthwort family, 156
biscuitroot, 184–85, 200
bistort, 18–19
bittersweet, 186–87
black cohosh, 182
Blackfeet Indians, 12, 18, 43, 46, 62,
    96, 124, 166, 172, 184, 206
bladder: disease, 130; inflammations,
    110; irritations of, 132
bleeding, 12, 19, 43, 58, 72, 108, 144,
    158, 162; emergency treatment of,
    148; following afterbirth; 60;
    internal, 94, 208; menstrual, 134;
    urinary tract, 60, 72. *See also* styptic
    agents; blood
blistering, 158
blood: coagulants, 158; pressure, 24;
    purifiers, 24, 60, 124, 152; sugar
    levels, 80, 142; thinning effects,
    164. *See also* hemostatic agents;
    alteratives, blood
blue camas, 20–21, 194
bluebells, 32, 68
boils, 188, 192
bone fractures, 76, 172
Borage family, 32, 78, 198
Boraginaceae, 32, 78, 198
Brassica nigra, 158–59
breast feeding, weaning infants from,
    128
bronchial congestion, 14, 66, 158. *See
    also* expectorants; respiratory
    system
bronchitis, 66, 68, 76, 90, 170, 186
bruises, 68, 118, 172, 180
Buckthorn family, 26, 126
buckwheat, 170
Buckwheat family, 18, 134, 168
buffalo berry, 20–21
bugleweed, 22–23, 28
bunchberry, 22–23, 124
burdock, 6, 24–25
burns, 29–30, 36, 62, 72, 78, 98, 118,
    132, 140, 146, 160, 162, 199

Buttercup family, 40, 182, 190, 192, 206
buttercups, 154

Cactaceae, 118
Cactus family, 118
calcium, 76, 210
California poppy, 26–27
Caltrop family, 44
camas, blue, 20–21, 194
camas, death, 20, 160, 194–95
Camassia quamash, 20–21, 194
Campanula americana, 69
    rotundifolia, 68
    species, 32, 68–69
Campanulaceae, 68
cancer, 4, 44, 50, 97, 108
cancerous lesions, 68
candidiasis, 62, 142
candyflower, 98–99
cankerroot, 40
capillary constrictor, 108
Caprifoliaceae, 54
Capsella bursa-pastoris, 158–59
caraway, 166
carbohydrates: assimilable, 166
cardiac: antispasmodic, 186; sedative,
    186, 198, 206; stimulant, 196. *See
    also* heart
cardiogenic toxin, 196
Carduus nutans, 144–45
carminative, 18, 28, 60, 102, 110,
    156, 160
Carophyllaceae, 30
cascara sagrada, 26–27
Castilleja species, 82–83
castor bean, 188–89
castor oil, 188
cataract, 206
cathartic, 27. *See also* laxatives
catkin-type flowers, 12
catnip, 28–29
cattail, 28–29, 98
Ceanothus velutinus, 21, 126–27
Centaurea cyanus, 88
    maculosa, 88–89
    pratensis, 88
    repens, 88
Cerastium species, 30
ceremonial herb blend, 124

ceremonial smudge, 208
chamomile, 110
chaparral, 44–45
cheeseweed, 94
Chenopodiaceae, 88
Chenopodium album, 88–89
    ambrosioides, 88
chest: colds, 34, 38; pains, 102
Cheyenne Indians, 102, 199
chickweed, 6, 30–31
chicory, 32–33
childbirth, 118, 206. *See also* postpar-
    tum
Chimaphila species, 120, 132
    umbellata, 110–11
chiming bells, 32–33
Chippewa Indians, 82, 108
chittam bark, 26
chlorophyll, 1
chokecherry, 34-35
cholesterol: blood, 160; reduction of,
    112
chronic depression, 3, 130
Chrysanthemum leucanthemum, 106–7
Cichorium intybus, 32–33
Cicuta douglasii, 142, 178, 214–15
Cimicifuga elata, 182
circulatory diseases, 166
Cirsium vulgare, 144–45
clasping pepperweed, 158
Claytonia bellidifolia, 138
    lanceolata, 138–39
    megarhiza, 138
Claytonia species, 138–39. *See also*
    Montia cordifolia
cleavers, 36–37
Clematis columbiana, 190–91
    ligusticifolia, 190
clove oil, 42
clover, red, 124–25
coagulants, 158
cocklebur, 24
codeine, 90
coffee substitute, 32, 48
cold remedies, 166
colic, 162
coltsfoot, 38–39, 98
columbine, 192–93
comfrey, 8, 78

Common Fern family, 94
Compositae, 6, 24, 32, 38, 48, 52, 66,
    88, 106, 108, 110, 116, 132, 144,
    166, 180, 208, 212
coneflower, 52–53
Conium maculatum, 184, 200–201, 204
conjunctivitis, 162
connective tissue injuries, 76
constipation, 21, 97, 134. *See also*
    laxatives
contraceptives, 64, 84, 97, 144, 199
contusions. *See* bruises
convulsions, 136, 202
coptis, 40–41
Coptis groenlandica, 40
    occidentalis, 41
    triflora, 40
cordage, 16, 172
corn lily, 198
Cornaceae, 22, 124
cornic acid, 124
cornine, 22
Cornus canadensis, 22–23
    stolonifera, 124–25
cortisone, 90
cottonwood, black, 114
cough, 14, 22, 34, 38, 56, 58, 68, 74,
    94, 132; drops, 74; suppression
    medicines, 90
coumarin, 102, 124
cow parsnip, 42–43
cramping, 178
cranesbill geranium, 42–43
Crassulaceae, 140
Crataegus douglasii, 70–71
Cree Indians, 46, 163
creeping bellflower, 68
creeping Charlie, 68
creosote bush, 44–45
Cruciferae, 154, 158
cucumber, wild, 146
cudweed, 108
Cupressaceae, 84
Cupressus, 84
curly dock, 169
currant, 12, 46–47, 56
cuts, minor, 62, 160
cyanide poisoning, 9
cymarin, 196

Cynoglossum officinale, 78–79
cypress, 84
Cypress Family, 84
cystitis, 72, 110
cystoliths, 210

daisy, oxeye, 106–7
dandelion, 32, 48–49, 116, 132
Datura stramonium, 202–3
death camas, 20, 160, 194–95
decongestants, 170. *See also* respira-
    tory system
delirium tremens, 136
demulcent, 30, 58, 94, 118
dermatitis, 54, 144, 156, 166; contact,
    42, 188, 208, 210, 212. *See also* skin
devil's club, 50–51
diabetes, 3, 46, 80, 144; adult onset,
    50, 84; juvenile onset, 118
diaphoretic, 54, 102, 108, 156, 166
diarrhea, 8, 27, 29, 34, 42–43, 54, 70,
    72, 130, 134, 162–63
dietary fiber, 112
digestion: aids, 142, 158
digestive system, 94; antispasmodic,
    42, 60, 110; damage to, 212;
    disorders, 29, 104, 124, 163, 178;
    fungal infections, 142; irritations,
    43, 56, 86, 112, 152, 169; irritations
    and arthritis, 172; parasitic
    infections, 208 (*see also* worms);
    tonic, 12, 169; ulcerations, 70
digitalis, 196
diuretic, 22, 30, 32, 36, 48, 54, 60, 66,
    76, 84, 86, 100, 106, 110, 118, 152,
    158, 160, 162, 166, 196
dock, 19
Dodecatheon species, 136
dogbane, 196–97
Dogbane family, 108, 196
dogtooth violet, 64
Dogwood family, 22, 124
dong quai, 178
douche, vaginal, 128
dye, 134
dysentery, 130

ear infections, 102
eardrops, 134

earth regenerator, 62, 102
Easter pudding, 19
echinacea, 52–53
Echinacea angustifolia, 52
   pallida, 52
   purpurea, 52–53
eczema, 46, 54
edibility, 7
Elaeagnaceae, 20
elderberry, 54–55
elephant's-head, 92
emetic, 27; herbs, 8, 54, 152
emmenogogue, 72
emollient, 30, 70, 94, 118
emotional children, 58
enema, 96
epazote, 88
epilepsy, 42, 136
Epilobium angustifolium, 62–63
   latifolia, 62
Equisetaceae, 76
Equisetum arvense, 76–77
   hyemale, 76–77
Ericaceae, 80, 86, 110, 120, 132
Eriodictyon angustifolium, 170
   californicum, 170
   crassifolium, 170–71
   trichocalyx, 170
Erodium cicutarium, 60–61
erosion, 102
Erythronium grandiflorum, 64–65
   montanum, 64
   oregonum, 64
   revolutum, 64
Eschscholzia californica, 26–27
estrogenic actions, 199
Euphoriaceae, 188
evening primrose, 46, 56–57; oil, 56
Evening Primrose family, 62
expectorant, 14, 16, 38, 50, 68, 74, 97,
   108, 152, 160, 166, 170, 184
eyes: disorders of, 88; examinations
   and surgeries, 186; inflammation
   of, 162; irritations of, 140; sore, 110
eyewash, 110, 134

facial scrub, 76
false hellebore, 58, 146, 198–99
false Solomon's seal, 58–59, 146, 198

fatty acid imbalances, 56
fawn lily, 64
female reproductive system, 198;
   disorders of, 178; tonics, 122, 162
Fern family, Common, 94
fevers, 60, 64, 114, 134, 204; herbs
   that lower, 164. *See also* analgesics
field chickweed, 30
field mint, 28, 60–61
filaree, 42, 60–61
fireweed, 6, 62–63
fishing line, 112
flavonoids, 22, 136
floral fillers, 16
flowering cycles, 7
flu and cold remedy, 66
formic acid, 210
Fourth of July flower, 130
Fragaria virginiana, 162–63
fragrene, 122
Fritillaria pudica, 168–69
fungal infections, 52, 148. *See also*
   candidiasis; digestive system

Gaia, 1, 4
Galium aparine, 36–37
   boreale, 36–37
gallbladder, 26
gamma linolenic acid, 46, 56
gastritis, 70
gastroenteritis, 180
gastrointestinal irritation, 134
Gaultheria shallon, 133
   species, 132
Geraniaceae, 42, 60
geranium, sticky wild, 42
Geranium family, 42, 60
Geranium viscosissimum, 42–43
giant hyssop, 28, 102
giardia, 154
gin, 84
ginger, wild, 156–57
gingerroot, 156
Ginseng family, 50
glacier lily, 64–65, 154, 198
Glecoma hederacea, 68–69
Glycyrrhiza lepidota, 90–91
glycyrrhizin, 90
Gnaphalium, 108

goatsbeard, 132
goldenrod, 66–67
goldenrod yellow dye, 104
goldenseal, 40
goldthread, 40
gooseberries, 46
Gooseberry family, 46
Goosefoot family, 88
gout, 186
gram-positive bacteria, 148
gromwell, 198–99
Grossulariaceae, 46
ground ivy, 68–69
grouse-wortleberry, 80
guidelines, commonsense, 9
gums: discomforts of teething in
    children, 76; anesthetic for, 42

hair: promotion of growth, 196; rinse,
    76, 94; reduction of loss of, 172
hallucinations, 202
harebell, 32, 68
hawthorn, 70–71
hay fever, 66, 163
headaches, 34
heal-all, 70–71
healing, herbs that promote. *See*
    vulnerary
healing wash for external wounds, 108
heart: disease, 34, 56, 164; palpitations,
    192; sedative, 86, 206; tonics, 70,
    100, 102
heartburn, 110, 132, 162, 204
Heath family, 80, 86, 110, 120, 132
hedge nettle, 28, 72–73
hell's bells, 202
hemlock parsley, 184, 200–201, 204
hemorrhage. *See* bleeding
hemorrhoids, 86, 120, 188
hemostatic, 22, 43, 106
henbane, black, 8, 186–87, 202
henbit, 72–73
hepatic diseases, 44
hepatitis, 3, 40
Heracleum lanatum, 42–43
herpes, 3
Heuchera species, 12–13
HIV, 3, 40
holly, 104

Honeysuckle family, 54
horehound, 22, 74–75
horsemint, 102
horsetail, 76–77
hound's tongue, 78–79
huckleberry, 80–81
hydrocyanic acid, 9, 34, 54
Hydrophyllaceae, 154, 170
Hydrophyllum capitatum, 154–55
hyoscyamine, 202
Hyoscyamus niger, 186–87
hyperactive children, 26
hyperglycemia, 118
Hypericaceae, 130
hypericin, 130
Hypericum anagalloides, 130
    formosum, 130
    perforatum, 130–31
hypertension, 70; plants which may
    cause, 90
Hypochaeris radicata, 48
hypotensives, 70, 100, 108, 126,
    198–99
Hyssopus officinalis, 102
hysteria, 136

Ilex opaca, 104
immunostimulant, 16, 52, 148
Indian paintbrush, 82–83
Indian tobacco, 6
Indians, herbal use by. *See specific*
    tribal names
indigestion, 88
infections: bacterial, 3, 52, 148;
    postpartum, 60
influenza, 40, 54
insanity, 58, 163
insect: bites, 12, 42, 72, 120, 140, 154,
    162, 164; repellent, 166
insecticides, 106, 198, 212
insomnia, 150
intestinal gas, 156
Inuit Indians, 92
Ipomoea species, 202
iron, 24, 48, 168, 210
ivy, ground, 68–69

jams, 54
jaundice, 88, 212

jellies, 34, 46, 54
jimsonweed, 202–3
Johnny-jump-up, 152
joint injuries, 172
juniper, 84–85
Juniperis commonis, 84–85
    occidentalis, 84
    osteosperma, 84–85
    scopulorum, 84

kidney: 76; disorders of, 46; stones,
    97, 110; tonics, 60, 66; weak, 212
kinnikinnick, 132, 86–87
Klein, Robyn, 214
knapweed, 88–89
lamb's quarter, 88–89
knotweed, 18

Labiatae, 18, 22, 28, 60, 68, 70, 72,
    74, 100, 102, 128, 136, 208
Lactuca serriola, 48, 116–17
Lakota Indians, 102, 199
lamb's quarter, 88–89
Lamium amplexicaule, 72–73
    maculatum, 72
    purpureum, 72
Larrea tridentata, 44–45
lavender hyssop, 102
laxative, 22, 26, 32, 54, 58, 62, 112,
    124, 146, 152, 166, 183
lead poisoning, 169
Leguminosae, 90, 124
Leonurus cardiaca, 100–101
Lepidium perfoliatum, 158–59
lettuce, wild, 48
lettuce opium, 116
Levisticum officinale, 204
lice, 172
Lichen family, 14
licorice, 90–91
Ligusticum canbyi, 204–5
    porteri, 204
    species, 200, 204–5
    tenuifolium, 204
Liliaceae, 16, 20, 58, 64, 146, 160,
    168, 172, 194, 198
lily, glacier, 64–65, 154, 198
Lily family, 16, 20, 29, 58, 64, 112,
    146, 160, 168, 172, 194, 198

lion's heart, 100
Lithospermum arvensis, 199
    ruderale, 199
    species, 198–99
liver: cellular regeneration, 144;
    damage to 144, 212; disorders of,
    104; dysfunction, 24; fatty acid
    imbalances in, 56; herbs that may
    cause damage to, 44; stimulants, 32,
    134, 168; tonics, 24, 124, 144
Lomatium cous, 184
    dissectum, 184–85
    species, 184–85, 200
    triternatum, 184–85
lotions, 70
lousewort, 92–93
lovage, 178, 204
lower blood pressure. *See* hypotensives
lupeol, 12
Lycopus americanus, 22–23
    asper, 22
    unifloris, 22
lymphatic system: disorders of, 12;
    tonic, 36, 126

Madder family, 36
Mahonia species, 104
maidenhair fern, 94–95
male impotency, 160
mallow, 94–95
Mallow family, 94
Malva neglecta, 94–95
Malvaceae, 94
manganese, 210
manzanita, 86
Marrubium vulgare, 22, 74–75
marsh mallow, 94
Matricaria matricarioides, 110–11
mayweed chamomile, 110
meadowsweet, 96–97
menopausal discomforts, 178, 182
menstrual: bleeding, 72, 132; cramp-
    ing, 182; cycle suppressant, 199;
    disorders, 178; flow regulator, 210;
    stimulant, 94
Mentha arvensis, 60
    piperita, 60
menthol, 60

Mertensia bella, 32
  ciliata, 32
  longiflora, 32
  oblongifolia, 32–33
  paniculata, 32
  perplexa, 32
  species, 32–33, 69
metabolic dysfunctions, 46
metals, heavy, 76, 169
methyl salicylate, 96
microclimates, 7
migraine headaches, 72, 108, 190
milk production, stimulation of, 144
milk thistle, 144
milkweed, 96–97
Milkweed family, 96
Mimulus guttatus, 98–99
mind-enhancer, 50
minerals, 122
miner's lettuce, 98–99
mint, field, 28, 60–61
Mint family, 22, 28, 60, 68, 70, 72, 74,
  100, 102, 128, 136, 208; plants that
  look like, 14
Mohawk Indians, 108
Monarda didyma, 18
  fistulosa, 18–19
monkeyflower, 14, 98–99
Montia (Claytonia) cordifolia, 98–99
  perfoliate, 98–99
morning glory, 202
motherwort, 100–101
motion sickness, 202
mountain sweetroot, 182
mouth: anesthetics for, 42; inflammations of, 120, 126, 163; irritations
  of, 126; open sores of, 40
mouthwash, 18; disinfectant, 128
mucilage, plant, 56, 94, 112, 140
mucous membranes, 108
mucus, secretions of, 106, 170
mule's ears, 16
mullein, 102–3
multiple sclerosis, 136
muscle: aches, 68, 162; liniment, 180;
  relaxant, 92; tension, 150
musk thistle, 144
mustard, black, 158
Mustard family, 154, 158

mustard plaster, 158

nausea, 34, 54
Nepeta cataria, 28–29
nervine, 88
nervous system: disorders, 190;
  infections, 130; injuries, 130, 136;
  tonics, 136
nervous tension, 136
nettle, 19, 102, 210–11
Nettle family, 210
nettle, hedge, 28, 72–73
nettle-leafed horsemint, 102–3
nettle, purple dead, 72
nettle, stinging, 102, 210–11
Nevada Indians, 82
Nicholas Culpeper, 88
Nightshade family, 186, 202
Nootka Indian, 20
northern bedstraw, 36
nursing mothers, 144
nutritive tonic, 14, 24, 124, 162, 210

Oenothera biennis, 56–57
  subacaulis, 56
  tanacetifolia, 56
ointments, 30, 70
Ojibwa Indians, 58, 60, 92
old man's beard, 148
Onagraceae, 56, 62
onion, wild, 160–61, 194
opium poppy, 26
Oplopanax horridum, 50–51
Opuntia fragillis, 118
  species, 118–19
orchid, 29
oregano, wild, 18
Oregon grape, 104–5
Origanum species, 18
osha, 200, 204–5, 214
Osmorrhiza chilensis, 142–43, 182
  occidentalis, 142–43
Oswego tea, 18
otehimika, 163
ovarian cysts, 126, 188
oxalic acid, 134, 168
oyster leaf, 32
oyster root, 132
oxeye daisy, 106–7

Panax quinquefolius, 50
pansy, 152
Papaveraceae, 26
paralysis, 108, 199, 206
parasitic infections, 144, 208. *See also* worms
parasitic plants, 92
Parneliaceae, 148
parsley, hemlock, 184, 200–201, 204
Parsley family, 42, 142, 166, 178, 184, 200, 204, 214
parsnip, cow, 42–43
pasqueflower, 206–7
Pea family, 90, 124
pearly everlasting, 108–9
Pedicularis contorta, 92–93
    groenlandica, 92–93
pemmican, 134
penicillin, 148
pepper substitute, 84, 158
pepper vine, 190
peppermint, 60
pepperweed, clasping, 158
Perideridia gairdneri, 166–67
periwinkle, 108–9
Petasites frigidus var. *nivalis,* 38
    palmatus, 38–39
    sagittata, 38
petiole, 12
photosensitivity, plant-caused, 130
photosynthesis, 1
physical overexertion, 92
phytosterols, 186
pigweed, 14
pillow stuffing, 36
pineapple weed, 110–11
Pink family, 30
pipsissewa, 110–11, 120, 132
Plantaginaceae, 112
Plantago elongata, 112
    major, 112–13
    patagonica, 112
    psyllium, 112
Plantain family, 112–13
pneumonia, 68; viral, 38
pneumococcus, 148
poison: antidotes for, 22, 27; arrows, 198; paralytic fish, 102
poison hemlock, 200

poison oak, 12
pollution, 76
Polygonaceae, 18, 134, 168
Polygonum bistortoides, 18–19
Polypodiaceae, 94
polysaccharide, 148
poplar, 96, 114–15
Poppy family, 26
Populus tremuloides, 114–15
    trichocarpa, 114–15
Portulacaceae, 98, 138
postpartum: infections, 60; swelling, 86, 120; tonic, 210
pot scrubber, 76
potassium, 210
potentially toxic alkaloids, 92
poultice, 42, 56, 58
prairie sagewort, 208
premenstrual syndrome, 46, 56
prickly lettuce, 48, 116–17
prickly-pear cactus, 118–19
Primrose family, 136
Primulaceae, 136
prince's pine, 110
prostate, inflammatory diseases of, 172
protein, 48
Prunella vulgaris, 70–71
Prunus virginiana, 34–35
pseudohypericin, 130
psyllium, 112
purple coneflower, 52–53
Purslane family, 98, 138
pussy willows, 164
pussytoes, 108
pyrethrins, 106
pyrola, 110, 120–21
Pyrola asarifolia, 120–21
    secunda, 120
    uniflora, 120

quaking aspen, 114–15

ragweed, 66
Ranunculaceae, 40, 182, 190, 192, 206
Ranunculus family, 142
rashes, 42
raspberry, 122–23, 162
red osier dogwood, 22, 124–25
red root, 21, 126–27

redroot amaranth, 14
refrigerant, 30
repellent, 62
respiratory system, 94; antiviral, 184, 204; arrest, 202; congestion, 102, 144; demulcent, 58; hemorrhage, 102; stimulant, 50
Rhamnaceae, 26, 126
Rhamnus caroliniana, 26
purshiana, 26–27
rheumatoid conditions, 24, 32, 82, 92, 172, 186, 199, 206
Ribes aureum, 46–47
glandulosum, 46
hudsonianum, 46
species, 12, 46–47
Ricinus communis, 188–89
ringworm, 188
Rorippa nasturtium-aquaticum, 154–55
Rosa woodsii, 162–63
Rosaceae, 34, 70, 96, 122, 134, 162
Rose family, 34, 70, 96, 122, 134, 162
rose hips, 162
rose-petal wine, 162
rotenone, 102
roundworms, 89
rubber, 116
Rubiaceae, 36
Rubus idaeus, 122–23
parviflorus, 122–23
Rumex acetosella, 134-35
crispus, 168–69
obtusifolius, 168
occidentalis, 168
sangineus, 168
venosus, 168

sage, 128–29, 170, 208
sagebrush, 7, 208–9
sageweed, 208
sagewort, 208
Saint John's Wort family, 130
salal, 132–33
Salicaceae, 114, 164
salicin, 114
salicylates, 96, 164
Salix geyeriana, 165
species, 164–65
salsify, 132, 133
salt substitute, 38

salves, 30, 70
Salvia apiana, 128–29
leucophylla, 128
mellifera, 128
munzii, 128–29
officianalis, 128
species, 128–29, 208
Sambucus callicarpa, 54
cerulea, 54–55
mexicana, 54
racemosa, 54
saponin, 20, 152, 172
Saxifragaceae, 12
Saxifrage family, 12
scoot berries, 146
scopolamine, 202
Scotch harebell, 68
scouring rush, 76
Scrophulariaceae, 14, 82, 92, 98, 102
scurvy, 19, 89, 134
Scutellaria argentea, 136
canadensis, 136
galericulata, 136
scutellarin, 136
sedative, 22, 26, 28, 92, 100, 102, 108, 110, 116, 136, 150, 152, 206; cardiac, 186, 206
Sedum lanceolatum, 140
oregonense, 140–41
stenopetalum, 140–41
selenium, 82
self-heal, 70
serviceberry, 134–35
shampoo, 128
sheep sorrel, 134–35, 168
Shepherdia argentea, 20
canadensis, 20
shooting star, 136–37
Shoshone Indians, 199
silica, 76
Silybum marianum, 144
silymarin, 144
Sitka alder, 12
sitz bath, 86
skin: cancer, 134; circulatory impairments of, 156; disorders, 24, 186; eruptions, 190; irritations of, 18–19, 29–30, 36, 42, 58–62, 94, 98, 118, 140, 146, 164; wash, 12, 54, 128, 208

skullcap, 14, 22, 136–37
sleep aid, 116
Smilacina racemosa, 58–59
    stellata, 58–59
smoking mixtures, herbal, 86, 124
smudge, 128, 208
snakebite, 52, 97
soap, 172
Socrates, 214
Solanaceae, 186, 202
Solanum dulcamara, 186–87
Solidago canadensis, 66–67
    gigantea, 66
    multiradiata, 66
    occidentalis, 66
Sonchus species, 48–49
Songish Indians, 98
sowthistle, 48
spastic colon, 26
speedwell, 14–15, 136
spinach, 9, 169
Spiraea betulifolia, 97
    species, 96
Spotted cat's ear, 48
sprains, 172, 180
spring beauty, 138–39
Spurge family, 188
Stachys palustris, 72–73
Stellaria media, 30–31
steroids, 90; plant, 186
stimulants, 18; appetite, 80
stinging nettle, 102, 210–11
stomach: disorders of, 96, 134; ulcers,
    90, 92; upset, 60, 110, 156
stomachache, 89, 144, 204
Stonecrop family, 140–41
storksbill, 60
strawberry, wild, 162
streptococcus, 148
Streptopus amplexifolius, 58, 146–47
styptic agent, 19, 66, 120
sunburn, 58
Sunflower family, 6, 16, 24, 32, 38,
    48, 52, 66, 88, 106, 108, 110, 116,
    132, 144, 166, 180, 208, 212
sunscreen, 44
suture material, 112
sweet Cicely, western, 142
sweetroot, 142–43, 182, 214
Symphytum species, 78

syphilis, 206
syrup, 34

Tanacetum vulgare, 212–13
tangleweed, 36
tannic acid, 86, 134, 169
tannins, 12
tansy, 212–13
Taraxacum officinale, 48–49
thiaminase, 76
Thimbleberry, 122–23
thistle, 144–45
thorny buffalo berry, 20
thread, 112
throat: infections, 18; irritations of,
    34, 56, 72, 88, 120, 126, 140, 162,
    166, 198, 212
thujone, 166
tonics, preventative, 52
tonsillitis, 126
toxic substances in the body, 90
toxicity, plant, 8, 176–77
trace minerals, 48, 158
Tragopogon dubius, 132–33
    porrifolius, 132
    pratensis, 132
traveler's joy, 190
Trifolium pratensis, 125
    species, 124
tuberculosis, 3 12, 69, 76, 108, 132,
    148
tumors, 44, 134; cancerous growth
    inhibitor, 108; fibroid, 126. *See also*
    antitumor
twisted-stalk, 58, 146–47, 198
tymol, 18
Typha angustifolia, 28
    latifolia, 28–29
Typhaceae, 28

ulcers, 54, 90, 192; external, 130
Umbelliferae, 42, 142, 166, 178, 184,
    200, 204, 214
United States pharmacopoeia, 12
urethritis, 72
uric acid, excess, 158
urinary tract: astringents, 76, 84, 110;
    bleeding, 60; disorders of, 80, 90,
    120, 172; incontinence, 102;
    irritations of, 43, 76, 86, 92, 210

ursolic acid, 70
Urtica dioica, 210–11
   species, 102, 210–11
Urticaceae, 210
usnea lichen, 148–49
Usnea species, 148–49
uterus: antispasmodic and tonic, 100;
   disorders of, 46
uva-ursi, 86–87

vaccines, 3
Vaccinium globulare, 80–81
   membranaceum, 80
   scoparium, 80
vaginal douche, 96
valerian, 150–51
Valeriana edulis, 150
   sitchensis, 151
Valerianaceae, 150
varicosity, 166
vascular: diseases, 56; tonics, 166
vasoconstrictor, 108, 158, 196
vasodilators, 156, 180
venereal disease, 96, 97, 144
venomous bites, 88
Veratrum californicum, 198
   viride, 198–99
Verbascum thapsus, 102–3
Veronica americana, 14–15
   species, 14–15, 136
Vinca major, 108–9
   minor, 108
Viola adunca, 153
   arvensis, 152
   canadensis, 153
   orbiculata, 153
   tricolor, 152
Violaceae, 152
violet, 152–53
virgin's bower, 190
viruses, 3; retro-viruses, 130
visual weakness, 32
vitamins, 122, 168; **A,** 134, 158, 210;
   B, 158; **B-1,** 76; **C,** 19, 62, 80, 104,
   114, 134, 158, 162, 210; **D,** 210; **E,**
   48

vomiting, herbs to induce, 8, 54, 152
vulnerary, 70, 72, 88, 114, 130

wahpé yatápi, 102
warts, 97, 118
watercress, 14, 98, 154–55
water hemlock, 42, 142, 178, 214
water horehound, 22
waterleaf, 154–55
Waterleaf family, 154, 170
water repellant, 62
water retention, 24, 32, 90
white sagewort, 208
whooping cough, 38, 62, 69, 186
willow, 96, 114, 124, 164–65
willow herb, 62
wine, 34, 54
Winnebago Indians, 18
wintergreen, 6, 120
worms, 34, 108, 130, 208, 212
wormwood, 128, 208
wort, wound, 66
wounds, 16, 72, 78, 112, 118, 130,
   148, 154, 199, 206; field dressings
   for, 154
wounds, minor, 162
Wyethia species, 16

Xanthium strumarium, 24
Xerophyllum tenax, 16–17

yampa, 166–67
yarrow, 163, 166–67, 212
yellow bells, 168–69
yellow dock, 134, 168–69
yerba santa, 170–71
yucca, 172–173
Yucca baccata, 172
   brevifolia, 172-73
   glauca, 172
   schidigera, 172–73

Zigadenus elegans, 20, 194
   venenosus, 194–95
   species, 160, 194–95
Zygophyllaceae, 44

Gregory L. Tilford

About the Author

An internationally renowned herbalist and naturalist, Gregory L. Tilford travels North America teaching about herbs and herbalism and lecturing at North America's top institutes of herbal study. Tilford is a member of the American Herbalist Guild and president of the Natural Pet Products Association. Author of *The EcoHerbalist's Fieldbook,* he is a contributing editor and herb advisor to *Natural Pet Magazine.* Tilford and his wife, Mary, own and operate Animals' Apawthecary, producers of herbal health care products for dogs and cats, in Conner, Montana.

Michael Moore, a leading authority on western herbs and herbalism, founded and now directs the Southwest School of Botanical Medicine in Bisbee, Arizona. He is the author of several popular books on herbal medicine, including *Medicinal Plants of the Mountain West, Medicinal Plants of the Pacific West,* and *Medicinal Plants of the Desert and Canyon West.*

239

FROM EARTH TO HERBALIST
An Earth Conscious Guide to Medicinal Plants

Gregory L. Tilford
With a Foreword by Rosemary Gladstar

❧262 pages
❧5⅜ x 8⅜
❧paper $21.00
❧ISBN 0-87842-372-9

"A breakthrough book. . . . Gregory challenges us to reconsider our roles as herbalists, to go beyond health care consultant, medicine-maker, wildcrafter, and gardener/farmer to become earth-steward herbalists, protectors of the wild gardens."

—Rosemary Gladstar, Founder of United Plant Savers

Picking up where other herb books leave off, *From Earth to Herbalist* guides budding and self-reliant herbalists in making and using plant medicines—while sounding an urgent call to preserve and protect vanishing wild plant species. Written by one of America's foremost herbalists, this unprecedented guide covers the common uses of over 125 species of North American medicinal plants. Fifty-two plant profiles feature crisp, color photographs and easy-to-understand instructions on how to identify, harvest, propagate, and process medicinal herbs. *From Earth to Herbalist* is a must for anyone interested in wild plant preservation and herbal medicine.

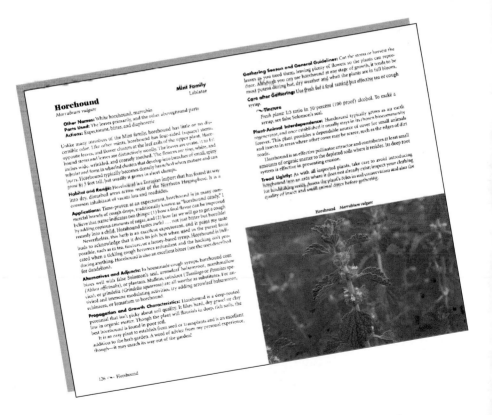

Available from your bookseller or call 1-800-234-5308 to order your copy of *From Earth to Herbalist* today!

We encourage you to patronize your local bookstore. Most stores will order any title they do not stock. You may also order directly from Mountain Press, using the order form provided below or by calling our toll-free, 24-hour number and using your VISA, MasterCard, Discover or American Express.

Some other Natural History titles of interest:

____A Field Guide to Nearby Nature	$15.00
____Birds of the Northern Rockies	$12.00
____Birds of the Pacific Northwest Mountains	$14.00
____Botany in a Day	$22.50
____Coastal Wildflowers of the Pacific Northwest	$14.00
____Desert Wildflowers of North America	$24.00
____Edible and Medicinal Plants of the West	$21.00
____From Earth to Herbalist *An Earth-Conscious Guide to Medicinal Plants*	$21.00
____An Introduction to Northern California Birds	$14.00
____An Introduction to Southern California Birds	$14.00
____Mountain Plants of the Pacific Northwest	$25.00
____Northern Flights	
Tracking the Birds and Birders of Michigan's Upper Peninsula	$12.00
____Northwest Weeds	
The Ugly and Beautiful Villains of Fields, Gardens, and Roadsides	$14.00
____OWLS Whoo are they?	$12.00
____Plants of Waterton-Glacier National Parks	
and the Northern Rockies	$14.00
____Raptors of the Rockies	$16.00
____Roadside Plants of Southern California	$15.00
____Sagebrush Country *A Wildflower Sanctuary*	$14.00
____Sierra Nevada Wildflowers	$16.00
____Watchable Birds of California	$18.00
____Watchable Birds of the Great Basin	$16.00
____Watchable Birds of the Rocky Mountains	$14.00
____Watchable Birds of the Southwest	$14.00
____Wild Berries of the West	$16.00

Please include $3.00 per order to cover shipping and handling.

Send the books marked above. I enclose $_____

Name_____

Address_____

City_____State_____Zip_____

☐ Payment enclosed (check or money order in U.S. funds)

Bill my: ☐ VISA ☐ MasterCard ☐ Discover ☐ American Express

Card No._____Exp. Date:_____

Signature _____

MOUNTAIN PRESS PUBLISHING COMPANY
P.O. Box 2399 • Missoula, MT 59806
Order Toll Free 1-800-234-5308 • Have your credit card ready.
e-mail: info@mtnpress.com • website: www.mountain-press.com